100 Years of
British Electric Tramways

E. Jackson-Stevens

David & Charles
Newton Abbot   London   North Pomfret (Vt)

British Library Cataloguing in Publication Data

Jackson-Stevens, E.
    100 years of British electric tramways.
    1. Electric railroads – Great Britain –
    Cars – History
    I. Title
    625'.66'0941   TF920

    ISBN 0–7153–8722–7

Phototypeset by
Northern Phototypesetting Co., Bolton
and printed in Great Britain
by Biddles Ltd., Guildford, Surrey
for David & Charles (Publishers) Limited
Brunel House, Newton Abbot, Devon

Published in the United States of America
by David & Charles Inc
North Pomfret, Vermont 05053, USA

Jacket illustration: Latest Blackpool tramcar delivered in
1985. (*Blackpool Corporation Transport*). *Front flap
illustration:* Blackpool tramcar of the late 1880s.

Contents

Introduction

One realises with something of a shock when attempting to discuss the characteristics of the erstwhile efficient electric tramcars, which graced the streets of Great Britain in the closing years of the last century and the first half of this one, that so very many people under the age of 30 or sometimes 40, have no knowledge whatever of the subject. It is salutary to remember in these days of acute traffic congestion in our cities where the ubiquitous motor car and the motor bus have succeeded in defeating their own primary purpose of transporting people quickly, that these same cities were once served by a clean, fumeless, swiftly accelerating and remarkably cheap form of transport, reliable and exceptionally competent.

In 1985 the centenary to mark the opening in Blackpool of the first electric tramway in Britain for fare-paying passengers is being commemorated and it is appropriate that a survey of the early struggles and subsequent successful achievements of this interesting form of transport and its vital service throughout two world wars should be recorded.

The commercial development and social interest of electric tramways is a subject of considerable magnitude, and my aim has been to arouse the interest of many who may never have enjoyed the pleasures of this mode of travel unless, of course, they have experienced it abroad where the electric tramcar, or Light Rail Transit (LRT) as it is now termed, still flourishes most successfully.

Scores of books and booklets have been written about various aspects of electric tramway systems in Britain, the latter dealing with individual towns and local undertakings both municipal and company owned, a total of 180 in all — 101 municipally owned and 79 company owned. In compiling this book it was apparent that to make it most helpful to those who did not have the good fortune to live in the 'electric tramway era' in Britain, I should concentrate on presenting a picture of an overall selection of the main representative characteristics and the problems encountered. Thus I have endeavoured, within limits, to describe the history and development over the past century of the electric tramway in Britain in its many forms with a view for the future.

In making a personal selection of tramway pictures, I have aimed at achieving a reasonable cross-section of Britain's electric tramways, including a high proportion of hitherto unpublished views, tapping many sources — newspaper libraries, local authorities, manufacturers, transport undertakings, commercial street views and private collections — and I would like to record my appreciation of their willing help.

E. JACKSON-STEVENS,
Glastonbury 1984

1

The Background of the Street Tramway

'Of all inventions, the alphabet and the printing press alone excepted, those inventions which abridge distance have done most for the civilization of our species. Every improvement in the means of locomotion benefits mankind morally and intellectually as well as materially, and not only facilitates the interchange of the various productions of nature and art, but tends to remove national and provincial antipathies, and to bind together all the branches of the great human family' – Lord Macaulay.

In 1776, a cast-iron tramway, nailed to wooden sleepers, was laid down at the Duke of Norfolk's colliery near Sheffield. The person who designed and constructed this line was John Curr, whose son erroneously claimed for him the invention of the cast-iron tramway but which he certainly had adopted. The plates of these early tramways were 'L' shaped to guide the wheels along the road.

In 1789 William Jessop constructed a tramway at Loughborough in Leicestershire and introducing the cast-iron edge-rail, with flanges cast on the tyre of the waggon-wheels to keep them on the track, instead of having the flange cast on the rail itself; this tyre was shortly afterwards

A South Staffordshire steam tramway locomotive and trailer tramcar on the Dudley–Handsworth route in 1893 before electrification. (*J. S. Webb*)

City of Birmingham Tramways Co open top cable car on Handsworth route about 1909. (*J. S. Webb*)

adopted in other places. In 1800 Benjamin Outram of Little Eaton, Derbyshire used stone instead of timber for supporting the ends of joints of the rails.

The growth of early tramways originated from necessity and was modified by experience. Progress, as in all departments of mechanics, was effected by the exertions of many men; one generation entering upon the labours of that which preceded it, carrying them onward to further stages of improvement, similarly the methods of locomotion improved. It was not the invention of one man, but of a succession of men, each working according to the needs of the period, each unravelling a succession of problems which were only to be solved after long and laborious efforts and experiments.

The same circumstances which led to the rapid extension of early tramways and railways to direct the attention of engineers to the development of the steam-engine as a useful instrument for motive-power; first for the haulage of coal and later, as its potentialities became more apparent, for the haulage of passengers on railways. Subsequently a steam tramway locomotive invented by John

Downes was put through various trials on the previously horse-operated tramway at Handsworth, Birmingham, during January 1876 hauling a passenger car. The success of this steam tramway locomotive and trials with other modified types on other horse operated tramways, resulted in their adoption for a decade throughout the country.

There were, however, numerous complaints mainly about the excessive emission of smoke and steam from the locomotives especially in built-up areas. As the dates for the renewal of the Board of Trade (the forerunner of the present Ministry of Transport) original seven-year licences for the use of steam drew near, the complaints of all kinds from both individuals and local authorities became more insistent.

Other methods of locomotion were tried, notable cable-traction and accumulator cars. The former operated by an endless cable in a duct between the rails, whereby a 'gripper' on the car engaged with the cable for propulsion, while the latter used heavy batteries which required frequent charging and never had much success because of

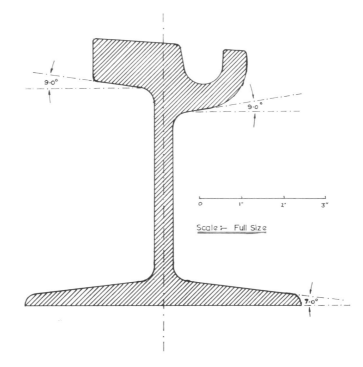

Crescent rail patented in 1860 which greatly helped the evolution of street tramways.

The first electric tramway locomotive constructed by Siemens & Halske running at the Berlin Exhibition in 1879. (*Siemens Museum, Munich*)

its restricted use.

Probably one of the greatest steps forward in the evolution of street tramways was the 'Crescent' rail patented in 1860. This was a rail sunk flush with the roadway which created a groove of such minor dimensions as to cause no inconvenience to other road users.

The next progressive step was the passing of the Tramways Act of 1870 which was more reviled than almost any other statute; although simplifying tramway projects many clauses were damaging to tramways. The most notable was 'that tramway undertakings, in addition to paving the roadway between the track gauge, must also pave and maintain the road surface for 18in on either side of their tracks'. This clause in the Act, was designed to recompense local authorities in the days of horse-drawn tramcars and was a burden which was never repealed even in the days of electric traction. Our legislators steadfastly refused to believe that tramcars were steam (and later electrically) propelled and made no use of the paving, despite the fact that electric tramcars ran right under their noses, hard by the Houses of Parliament, for half-a-century. This oppressive Act remains in force to this day and it had a considerable effect in the demise of tramways in Great Britain.

The first electric tramway was constructed by Siemens & Halske at the Berlin Exhibition in 1879.

It consisted of a four-wheeled electric locomotive drawing some small open cars each carrying six passengers. The locomotive was driven by a ring-wound geared motor and the current collected from a third rail, the running rails acting as return conductors, and it drew the small train round a section of the exhibition at a speed of 7 mph. This locomotive and one small car are now preserved in the German Transport Museum at Munich.

The first permanent electric tramway was built in Berlin in 1881, with a track length of $1\frac{1}{2}$ miles to metre gauge. It used what is today familiar to small-scale modern railway enthusiasts the world over, the two-rail system, in which the running rails and opposite wheels were insulated, one rail acting as a feeder and the other rail as a return current collector. The motor weighed $\frac{1}{2}$ ton and developed $5\frac{1}{2}$ horsepower with a line voltage of 90/100 volts. The car and passengers weighed about 5 tons. This system operated until 1893 when it was superseded by the overhead collection system.

The first electric tramway in Great Britain was built by Magnus Volk at Brighton in 1883. As in the Berlin electric tramway, the current for the motors was collected from two insulated running rails at 100 volts. This tramway is still in operation but the current is collected from a third rail with the return circuit through the running rails.

2

Electric Tramways, History and Development

Undoubtedly the first electric tramway in Great Britain to be operated for fare-paying passengers in a street was opened at Blackpool in September 1885, so to Blackpool belongs the credit for this enterprise which was to have a most remarkable impact from a travelling standpoint on the cities, towns and, indeed, developing suburbia and their inhabitants.

Blackpool's first system comprised a two-mile line on the Promenade, and the conduit system of operation was used whereby positive current was carried by two copper conductors inside a central channel and transmitted to the cars by a 'plough' underneath the cars. The original fleet of the Blackpool Electric Tramway Company amounted

to only ten cars, purchased at a cost of only £2,156. It was not possible to have a larger initial fleet as the output from the new generators, combined with considerable voltage loss through poor insulation, limited the number of cars which could be run.

Operating limitations were also imposed by the whole length of the track being single with loops every 300yd or so for cars to pass. The Company had set a flat fare of 2d (nearly 1p), thus reducing demand and giving electric car travel a certain 'status' as the horse buses only charged 1d. The hard seats and oil lamps for illumination with bad track and rudimentary springing for an electric car ride, was still preferable to the bumping and jolting

Laying the first rail on 13 March 1885 for the first British electric street tramway by Alderman MacNaughton, Chairman of Blackpool Tramway Committee. (*Stephen Palmer*)

horse buses. These early cars were equipped with a single motor of only seven horsepower, weighing 16cwt.

Even at this early stage of the development of the electric tramcar the heavy hand of oppressive bureaucracy, which bedevilled electric tramways in Great Britain throughout the whole time of their expansion, began to make itself felt. The Board of Trade (forerunner of the present Ministry of Transport) restricted their speed to 8mph although it is recorded that these conduit cars occasionally startled their lady passengers by bouncing down the Promenade at a rollicking 15mph!

The pioneer of Blackpool's electric tramway, Michael Holroyd Smith of Halifax who, together with Louis Crossley, another Halifax electrical engineer, had already built narrow-gauge and standard-gauge lines outside Mr Crossley's works at Cornbrook, Manchester with a track of 220yd and thus was undoubtedly the driving force behind the Blackpool enterprise. Holroyd Smith had influential friends on Blackpool Corporation and in 1884 he persuaded them to inspect the two

existing electric tramways, Volks Brighton line and Ireland's Giant's Causeway line but, singularly enough, they were not impressed. Some weeks later, on 3 October, he entertained them at Cornbrook where he had installed a full-size standard-gauge electric tramcar on his 110yd long track. This time they were considerably impressed and reported with enthusiasm to the Town Council on the merits of the vehicle and its performance.

'The movement of the car was everything that could be desired. Commencing with an almost imperceptible motion, free from the least jerk, it gradually increased in velocity until the maximum speed was obtained, when it was brought to a standstill again, either gradually, without the least jerk, or suddenly if required, within a distance equal to its own car length' was their verdict.

Following the Committee's visit to Manchester, things began to move quickly and the Corporation agreed that the new tenancy should be constructed on the system demonstrated at Cornbrook. Blackpool Electric Tramway Company was formed at the beginning of January 1885. Raising

9

One of the earliest surviving photographs of electric tramcars in Blackpool taken in 1886 or 1887. With their modern construction, front exits and electric lighting they could claim to being the most advanced electric tramcars in Britain at the time.

The original fleet was a modest 10 tramcars costing a mere £2,156. The Corporation took over the line in 1892 and because of trouble mainly with sand entering the conduits, converted to overhead-trolley wire operation in 1898–99. (*Stephen Palmer*)

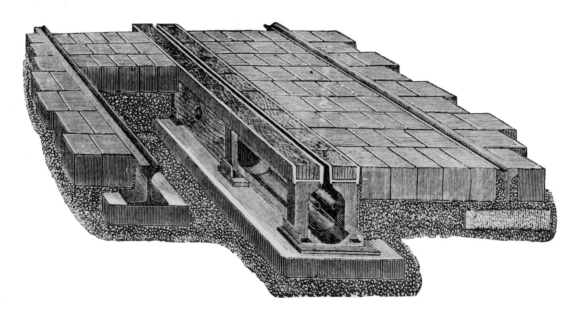

A cross-section of early Blackpool electric tramway track, showing the steel troughing above the centre conduit with the two copper conductors inside the channel itself. The channel was drained directly into the town drainage system. (*Stephen Palmer*)

the company's £30,000 nominal capital was no problem as applications for more than £50,000 came from all over the country.

On 13 March the first rail was laid, just north of Talbot Square, by Alderman MacNaughtan and Holroyd Smith attached the first insulator to the rail and work went ahead with remarkable speed. The Corporation was responsible for the roadbed, paving and the rails which were to be rented to the Tramway Company at $6\frac{1}{2}$% per annum while the Company itself had to provide the cars, build the depot and power-station and install the centre conduit, all under the control of Holroyd Smith. Work proceeded apace to such an extent that electric traction was officially inaugurated with much pomp and circumstance on 29 September 1885.

Holroyd Smith must take the major credit as the engineering of the line was largely his own creation but the Corporation also deserves praise for the support it gave him while the investors, who were

Between 1901 and 1903, 35 new double-deck cars were added to the fleet, including eight 'Dreadnought' bogie cars, illustrated, all open-top cars. The 'Dreadnoughts' were of a most unusual design with loading-steps extending the full width of the front and rear of the cars which tilted up to disclose the life-guard when the car was running in a foward direction. (*Stephen Palmer*)

11

A double-deck totally-enclosed Blackpool centre-entrance 94-seat tramcar under construction at English Electric works at Preston in 1934. These cars were of a very advanced design of which 14 were delivered to Blackpool Corporation and are still giving good service on its tramway, over 50 years later, having run over $1\frac{1}{4}$ million miles! (*English Electric-AEI Traction Ltd*)

prepared to back the enterprise to the extent of £50,000 in a proposition extremely speculative, are also to be commended. What finer testimony could there be to the enterprise of the three parties involved than the fact that Blackpool electric tramway is still operating today, the last conventional electric tramway in Great Britain and the oldest anywhere in the world?

The Blackpool enterprise provided the example on which the subsequent proliferation of electric tramways throughout Great Britain was constructed. Although the introduction of the electric street car made rapid strides elsewhere — there were 2,540 miles in the USA in 1896 — it was hampered in Britain by legislators whose inertia and want of imagination could not visualise much beyond the horse car, and continued to govern by statutes and regulations appropriate only to horses. Thus, by the end of the century, the mileage had increased from 779 in 1876 to only 1,040 and still worked mainly by horse or steam.

The real spurt in electrification occurred from 1900 to 1907, during which period the total mileage increased to 2,232 but thereafter the rate was slower and consisted chiefly of small additions to various systems. At the outbreak of the first world war in 1914 the mileage figure had reached 2,530 and many proposals then went into cold storage, some never to reappear, but a few others such as the reserved track sections at Birmingham, Liverpool and elsewhere were eventually built.

Unfortunately electric tramway development reached its zenith too late as the motor bus had developed contemporaneously with the electric tramcar. Improvements in the internal combustion engine were accelerated and facilities for making it were multiplied to meet the needs of military transport.

3
Bureaucratic Difficulties

In Great Britain electric tramway development was very slow from 1885 up to the early 1890s when the Leeds and South Staffordshire tramway systems were opened. The early delay was due partly to the opposition of local authorities – local councils being as devoted to myopia and obstructionism as they were at the advent of the early railways and as, indeed, they remain to this day towards any enterprise – and partly to the great expense and onerous conditions imposed on tramways which were constructed under the Tramways Act of 1870, a special Act of Parliament being necessary for each project.

The passage of the Light Railways Act of 1896, reduced the difficulty and the cost of obtaining powers to construct new tramways. Under this Act, tramways and light railways are broadly classified together and so far as the actual method of construction is concerned, an electric light railway could be, in many ways, merely an electric tramway constructed under the Light Railways Act of 1896.

The clause of the Act which crippled tramway working costs was the one whereby they were required to maintain the road surface for 18in on each side of the rails as well as the space within the track gauge. Tramway operators were therefore, (and still are) required to maintain many acres of road surface, to the relief of local rates but subsidising in later years the roadway for their competitors, the motor bus. However, this was only one of the restrictions.

Another section of the Act with a crippling effect on development during the electrification era provided that a local authority could, if it so wished, purchase a tramway compulsorily after 21 years or thereafter after every seven years. Naturally operators were loath to put fresh capital into their undertakings in these circumstances, and many lines continued to be worked by the original cars long after these should have been replaced by the more modern vehicles which were becoming available as advanced modifications were introduced.

It is necessary for any corporation or company constructing a tramway to 'obtain permission either from Parliament or the Light Railways Commissioners and plans showing the proposed route or routes must accompany the application, shewing the lengths of single and double track. A tramway authority must not open at one time a greater length than 100 yards of road which does not exceed $\frac{1}{4}$ mile in length and, in the case of any road exceeding this length a space of $\frac{1}{4}$ mile must be left between the openings. In no case is any part of the roadway to be left open for construction or repair work for a greater period than four weeks.'

The development of the British market and the manufacturing industry for electrical components for tramways was retarded by the tug-of-war and bickerings between municipal and private enterprise for the control of electric tramways. Most municipalities looked to their projected tramways to relieve their rates from the tramways profits and some wanted their tramways to produce a staple load to bolster over-ambitious electricity supply schemes where the municipality owned the local electric power station. Concerns like the British Electric Traction Company Ltd and its other subsidiaries were the chief protagonists on the other side; in many cases conditions were imposed on consents for a company to install a tramway in a town that it purchased the necessary electric power from the municipality instead of constructing its own power station. Municipal authorities were also jealous of local rights and boundaries.

Discords and obstructive or delaying tactics were rife, resulting in lack of co-ordination and many of the lines which were eventually built in large conurbations like London, Manchester and Birmingham could have had better tramway systems if local authorities had co-operated. Many local boundaries were regarded as sacrosanct and inviolate and an impediment to through running. Two big cities Bradford and Leeds meeting at the boundaries had different gauges although this was, in one instance, overcome in later years by constructing some of their cars with 'sleeve axles' able to expand and contract to accommodate to the 4ft 8½in Leeds gauge and the 4ft Bradford gauge but this was an isolated example. Halifax and the Woollen District of Yorkshire also had different gauges from Bradford. The East Ham

An early London United electric tramcar, No 112, at
Highgate.

and Ilford boundary lay a few hundred yards from
an important traffic point, but Ilford Council
would not, for years, allow through running. The
same applied to Croydon Corporation which
would not allow London County Council cars to
pass its boundary at Norbury for very many years
and Croydon cars could not therefore run into
London. There were many such inconsistencies,
due either to the intractability of neighbouring
authorities or to differences of gauge which
eventually gave the competing buses a big
advantage.

Municipal authorities often adopted a dog-in-
the-manger attitude towards private enterprise as
they were themselves deterred from building and
extending their own tramways. Under the terms of
their borrowing powers, the capital had usually to
be repaid within 21 or 30 years and any scheme
had to show a high operating revenue, whereas a
private company had only to find dividends on its
stocks and shares. Another aspect which impeded
the development of tramways was local politics, in
which the tramways became a tug-of-war between
opposing factions, similar to our railways since
1948 nationalisation, between the Socialists and
the Conservatives.

Due to the avaricious attitude of many local
councils, many proposals went into cold storage, a
majority never to appear again. The London
United Tramways Limited, operating in what were

then semi-rural suburbs of Acton, Chiswick and
Kew, promoted numerous further schemes and in a
spirit of optimism under its General Manager,
James Clifton Robinson (later knighted) who had
very expansive ideas, expanded Chiswick depot
and acquired some 340 passenger vehicles for
contemplated extensions. These were
subsequently baulked by Parliament's
unreasonable demands, which were sourly
commented on by the trade press at that time, and
it was found that only 150 tramcars of the new
fleet would be needed for its most intensive services
so the rest were sold. Local councils regarded the
newly formed tramway companies as milch-
cows for undertaking street-widenings; a
considerable number of these were done at the
expense of the companies but in many cases the
demands of the local authorities were so
financially outrageous and could not possibly be
complied with that the projected lines were,
therefore, never built.

The British Electric Traction Company Ltd
(BET), formed for the purpose of electrifying and
extending existing horse and steam tramways in
1895 throughout Great Britain was always
bedevilled by the ineptitude and incompetence of
local authorities, whose parochial outlook not only
retarded early progress to a considerable degree
but prevented many extensions materialising, to
the detriment of their towns and their residents.

The eventual Black Country system provided a typical example of the intransigent attitude encountered by this enterprising company which offered an overall plan for operating the whole of the electric tramway system throughout the Black Country, including the city of Birmingham, the neighbouring large towns of Wolverhampton, Dudley, West Bromwich and Walsall and the multitudinous small towns and settlements which comprised this closely-inhabited area.

It subsequently transpired that some towns built the tramways themselves and then leased them to BET to operate, some accepted municipal operation in its entirety, while yet other towns allowed BET to own and operate the trams within their boundaries. Many undertakings were small and localised and in some places too small to be economically viable as they could not obtain many of the economies available to the larger operations.

London County Council provided another example of a local authority's restrictive practice, by insisting on the conduit method of current collection, whereby a central slot rail between the track had to be installed because it was thought that the overhead trolley-wires would be unsightly; this was done on 123 miles of LCC's track with the remaining 43 miles at the outer sections in the suburbs being overhead equipped. Opposition to the erection of overhead wires, because it was thought they would ruin the skyline of the metropolis, put up the cost of electric tramway construction and maintenance to a level that only a capital city could be expected to afford. The

conduit lasted almost half a century and it is worth noting that when trolley-buses were introduced to London 40 years later the vastly more trolley-wires needed to operate this form of traction raised no objections! Conduit collection was costly, about double the cost of overhead wires.

Another method of current collection adopted by some towns, in an effort to placate fractious local authorities, was the 'stud contact' system whereby a series of spring operated studs were sunk into the roadway midway between the running rails and connected to an underground power cable. A 'skate' fitted under the car incorporating an electro-magnetic device, collected the current from the studs which only became 'live' while the car was actually passing over them; the skate was long enough to make contact with two studs at a time to maintain continuity. The studs were not unlike the present-day 'cats-eyes' on roadways. Immediately the skate broke contact with the studs by the passage of the car, they returned to their 'dead' position through the action of the spring. The only tramways using this method were Torquay, Mexborough, Lincoln, Hastings and Wolverhampton. This system was not very successful as occasionally there were cases of springs failing to return a stud to the neutral position and therefore remaining live and causing injury to pedestrians and horses, although Wolverhampton retained the system until 1921 when it replaced it with the overhead system.

4

The Edwardian Era

It is nowadays difficult to picture what our town roads must have been like in the horse tram days of Queen Victoria. Tarmac, concrete and woodblock surfaces had not been developed, and roads consisted of granite setts or cobblestones and water-bound macadam, the former only extending the necessary 18 inches outside the track, as required by the 1870 Act. Filth was usual, the excreta from hundreds of horses, including many working the trams, mixed with the mud or dust, according to the moods of the weather. A feature of our highways was the 'water-cart' used to spray

water on the dust during hot weather. Many electric tramways systems provided a tramway water-tank for the same purpose which was more efficient and quicker than the horse-drawn one it replaced.

Although the introduction of the electric street car had made rapid strides elsewhere, Great Britain had dragged its feet, mainly because of the bureaucratic difficulties previously explained.

The opposition to overhead wires had been a delaying factor to electrification up to the end of the last century but by the late 1890s the overhead

An early South Staffordshire Company electric tramcar, outside Pleck generating station, just before opening day on 21 November 1892.
(*J. S. Webb*)

trolley-wire had established itself and the succession of traction-poles supporting the wires was becoming an accepted part of our streets. The designers of traction-poles were determined that this new 'street furniture' should overcome the previous resentment and the standards and brackets were decorated with elaborate and elegant curved scrolls and spirals while the tops were crowned with heavy ornate finials.

With a rising population, improved passenger transport facilities were urgently needed. The overcrowded town and city centres of population could not adequately accommodate the workers and their families and access to outlying new suburban districts was imperative.

The economic need for the new electric car was overwhelming and the capital for the fixed equipment, power stations to generate the current, overhead trolley-wires and rolling stock was available. Electric tramcars were much cheaper to run in comparison with the horse car, the former being about 6d (2½p) per mile while the latter was 9d (3¾p) for the same distance although it soon became apparent that the cost of running an electric car fell sharply when the electric system was properly established. Once installed the advantages of the electric car soon became obvious; it used energy only while in motion, other than at night, when a minimal amount was required for the

lights, and electricity was supplied by a single power station to all the fleet whereas with the horse tram the high cost of maintenance was literally eating up the receipts from the fares. There was also the consideration that the electric car was larger, could carry more passengers and, moreover, it could be more highly utilised, easily accomplishing a hundred or more miles a day, more than twice the distance a horse could manage. Furthermore the electric cars were clean, fast, and comfortable, attracting an increasing number of passengers. The ratio of working expenses to receipts for horse tramways averaged over 80 per cent while electric trams brought this down to under 60 per cent.

At the dawn of the twentieth century where the horse and steam cars were already running the tracks had to be relaid with stronger rails to carry the heavier electric cars and in many cases its tentacles extended to areas where trams had never run before. Holes were dug in the pavements for the erection of the traction-poles, the maximum spacing then along the track was limited by law to 120 feet. They were embedded in 6ft of concrete and the height of the trolley-wire suspended from the traction-poles above the surface of the road was not allowed to be less than 20ft except under low bridges.

The supply and control of the electric current to

A tramway water car laying the dust in Aberdeen. In the early 1920s before tar-macadam roads became general, except for the tramway setts, the roads consisted of compacting stone, broken small and grouted in with sand and water, causing excessive dust on hot windy days. (*Aberdeen Corporation*)

17

A Worcester electric tramcar No 4 in 1904 on a test-run the day before the electric tramway was opened for public service. Note the oil-lamp casing mounted on the bulkhead, just above the man standing on the step. This remained alight when the trolley-pole was being turned round at termini and the car lights were, therefore, extinguished for a few moments.

the trolley-wires was by an underground cable feeder system which distributed it from the generating or sub-station to the working conductors. The trolley-wire potential was 550/600 volts dc and in compliance with regulations the wire was divided into half-mile sections insulated from one another; the connection with the feeder system was usually made at the centre or ends of each section.

In the conduit system, which had an insulated return, the negative feeders were duplicates of the positive feeders, but in the overhead system which had an earthed return, the negative system differed from the positive and required separate consideration. In Great Britain the feeder cables were laid underground except on very rural lines where like America, on the continent, and in the former Colonies they ran on the traction-poles.

Despite the bureaucracy town after town took to the electric tram as all the equipment of electrification appeared in the streets. After trial

runs and an inspection by the Board of Trade (from 1919 the Ministry of Transport) electric services commenced, usually accompanied by civic pomp and, in many cases, free rides for the populace on the first day.

The speeds attained by the new electric cars were much higher than the horse trams they replaced and steep gradients were no problem as the electric cars soon proved their capacity to work them with heavy loads.

The Edwardian era was a period when public utilities were being acquired by municipalities; water, gas and electricity and the tramways in many cases followed the same movement. Those who supported private enterprise claimed that the tramways should not be hampered by the bureaucracy of local government while the municipal advocates, on the other hand, thought that so important an undertaking as transport should not be left to the whims of speculative enterprise but should be run for the benefit of the town as a whole.

Because of the Tramways Act the scales were weighted so heavily against the companies that municipalisation was, in many cases, inevitable. The powers of veto, compulsory purchase and road maintenance all conspired to discourage private enterprise.

5
Basic Principles of a British Electric Tramcar

It seems incredible that a whole generation has grown up which never knew the electric tramcars which graced British streets for over half-a-century or, indeed, what a tramcar looked like or how it worked. There are electric tramcars still in use at Blackpool and the Isle of Man, and at the National Tramway Museum at Crich, Derbyshire, a comprehensive display of all kinds can be found. Other examples have been retained for local historical purposes at Covent Garden Museum, Birmingham Museum of Science & Technology, Bournemouth Transport Museum and several other museums. There is a half full size tramway in operation at Seaton, Devon, which runs from there to Colyton.

In Britain the electric tramcars were mainly double-deck, with single-deck cars being used on those systems which had light traffic or were subject to the restrictions of low railway bridges; the latter type were standard nearly all over the

world. Double-deck cars had the advantage of larger passenger capacity at the busiest hours at the expense of a certain amount of unnecessary weight during less busy times. A tramcar is a composite vehicle, the product of several firms, one firm constructing the motors, another the trucks or bogies, another firm the bodywork while the various components, controllers, hand-brake stocks, wheels, electrical equipment, life-guards, trolley-heads and a variety of other miscellanea came from a number of smaller firms, the ultimate vehicle being completed by one of the well-known tramcar builders.

Cars mounted on two bogies were known as double-truck cars or bogie-cars while those mounted on four-wheels were known as single-truck cars. The motors driving the cars were mounted adjacent to the driving wheels and the horsepower of the motors varied according to the weight of the car and the terrain of the district. For

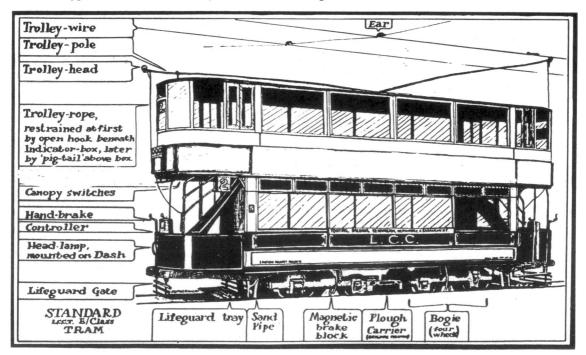

Sketch showing the basic principles of a standard type British electric tramcar.

normal terrain, a single-deck car would require two 25 or 35hp motors while a bogie-car would be equipped with anything from two 40hp up to two 70hp motors, depending on the gradients on the routes. On some very hilly routes, notably in London, a fleet of double-deck cars had equal-wheel bogies, each axle being equipped with a 35hp motor giving the car a total rating of 140hp, for greater adhesion.

What was known as 'maximum-traction' bogies were used considerably in Britain, consisting of two driving-wheels and two smaller pony non-driving wheels on each bogie, the object being to allow cars of greater length to be used, the extra non-driving wheels helping to distribute the weight, but essentially with most of the car weight on the driving axle of each bogie.

One of the most popular types of electric tramcar was the E/1 class; this was the standard tramcar used, with variations, throughout the country. Eventually no fewer than 1,050 of these were built for the London County Council and were the greatest number of cars of the same basic design ever constructed for one operator in Great Britain; additionally the neighbouring undertakings of Croydon, East Ham, West Ham and Walthamstow all had trams of the same design. They were mainly built by Hurst, Nelson & Co and the Brush Electrical Engineering Co Ltd of Loughborough, although a few were built by the London County Council itself at its Charlton works.

The illustration itemises the main characteristics of the E/1 Class car with explanatory notes. Starting from the top, the word 'ear' denotes the method of suspension of the 'trolley-wire'. On the roof of the car are the two 'trolley-poles' to collect the current, the one hooked down is out of use and would be released and used in the reverse direction with the other one now out of use hooked down. The 'trolley-head' was a globe-shaped swivelling brass head-casing containing a hard wearing phosphor-bronze trolley-wheel which rotated with the progress of the car. In later years graphite static 'skates' were used on some systems. The trolley-pole was held against the trolley-wire by means of trolley-base springs at a pressure of 15 to 25 pounds according

A maximum-traction type bogie car at Southend-on-Sea.

to local conditions and the speed of the cars. The 'trolley-rope' was attached near the head of the trolley-pole and was used by the conductor of the car to position the trolley-head on the overhead wire. The 'canopy switches' were circuit-breakers to interrupt the current to the motors in the event of an overloaded circuit or electrical fault; they were also used to make the car 'dead' when there was any necessity to take the casing off the controller in order to make adjustments to the equipment or, in the case of 'conduit' type current collection, to remove a faulty 'plough'.

The 'controller', as its name indicated, controlled the current to the motors to vary the speed of the car. The 'headlamp' was wired in conjunction with the tail red light and was reversed when the direction of the car was changed.

The 'lifeguards' are interesting as an example of the meticulous care exercised by the former Board of Trade in its anxiety to preserve human life in those days.

The 'gate' underneath the collision-fenders of the car actuated the 'tray' under the platform when it struck an obstruction, thus anyone knocked down by the car was prevented from being crushed by the wheels; no similar protection exists with present-day buses and coaches running on our roads. After being actuated, the lifeguard tray was re-set by a pedal on the driver's platform. The 'sandpipe' immediately behind the lifeguard tray was operated by another pedal by the driver's foot and was used to spray sand on the rails to assist adhesion when starting in wet weather or on greasy rails; it was also applied in an emergency stop if the wheels had locked and the car was skidding forward.

The 'hand-brake' applied the brakes to the wheels by means of a spindle turned with the brake-handle, this could be kept in the full-on position or at any intermediate point when the car was stopped or when descending long hills by means of a pawl which engaged with a ratchet and was operated by the driver's foot.

Between the wheels of each truck were the 'magnetic brake-blocks' which were also used to assist in stopping the car. Again this was a most interesting safety feature of electric tramcars, for in addition to the provision of mechanical brakes it was, and still is, a means of braking the car electrically. The method adopted was known as 'rheostatic braking' which acted independently of the supply of power to the car; braking was therefore available in the event of any failure either of the power supply or of contact between the collector (the trolley-pole, pantograph or conduit plough) and the conductor supplying the power. The controller had additional contacts which changed the connections to the motors in such a way that they acted as generators and their output was dissipated in the whole or part of the car starting-resistances, through which this current was passed.

The back electro-motive-force (EMF) of the motor opposed the flow of current through the armature from the line and if the motor was disconnected from the line but was kept revolving, the back EMF would set up a current in the opposite direction to the original motor-circuit, thus retarding the car. Additionally very effective braking was obtained by introducing magnetic-track-brakes into the circuit of the ordinary rheostatic brake. These magnetic track-brakes were designed for attachment to the car trucks and mounted immediately over the track-rails to which they were drawn down magnetically with considerable force. Two of these magnets were required for a single-truck car and four for a bogie-car. Magnetic braking was used as the 'service-brake' in the large cities such as London, Glasgow, Birmingham, etc for stopping cars but it was only used for emergency stops in many of the smaller systems because of the extra load thrown on to the motors by this method; larger motors were required otherwise smaller motors would overheat. Possibly smaller systems, with lighter cars thought that the extra expense involved in larger motors and equipment was not justified and they deemed the normal hand-brake sufficient to stop their cars.

The 'plough-carrier' illustrated on the London car was for the purpose of inserting the 'plough' to collect the current on the conduit systems.

It can be seen that the car illustrated was equipped with 'maximum-traction' bogies and also that it was of the basic original design. It underwent a number of modifications in later years, glass screens were fitted to protect the drivers from inclement weather – although one general manager of a smaller system, probably ensconced in the snug warmth of his office, refused to equip his cars with these screens saying that exposure to the elements was healthy for drivers! There were also interior improvements to this type of car. Originally when they were constructed the seating comprised longitudinal seats in the lower saloon and transverse reversable seats in the upper saloon, both of the slatted wooden type. In 1926, to increase comfort and speed, these cars appeared on the streets of London equipped with transverse, upholstered and reversable seats in both upper and lower saloons as well as the motors of a higher horse-power. They were then described as 'Pullman' type cars. To meet the increasing threat of motor-bus competition at this time many other systems followed London's example and 'Pullmanised' their fleets.

The initial rolling-stock was built to well-tried designs and these 'E' class cars lasted in many cases well over 40 years and did not look dated 30 years after the original models appeared. It should be borne in mind that the life of a tramcar was proven to be 40–50 years and there were cars running in Glasgow, at the abandonment of its system, which were even 60 years old, although they had been modernised several times but the bodies of the cars were the originals. The life of a modern motor bus is given as 12–20 years.

6

Early Types of British Electric Tramcars

The regional aspects of electric tramways were determined by the boundaries to which they were confined and also depended whether they were financed by the local municipality or were company owned. A number of engineering firms and tramcar builders quickly became geared to electric tramcar construction from 1899 onwards and standard productions were soon available.

At the same time, some specifications differed according to local needs which were many and varied. A district with a multiplicity of low railway bridges required single-deck cars for these routes while a large city system with a very intensive passenger-density needed larger cars with more powerful motors. In seaside localities or areas of picturesque scenery, open 'toastrack' tramcars were popular for summer working while in winter there was a demand for enclosing the upper decks

of 'open-topped' tramcars already in service and those on order.

A further regional consideration concerned the available capital. The larger municipally-owned electric tramways of London, Birmingham, Liverpool, Glasgow, Manchester and similar systems were better placed for modernising their fleets and keeping abreast of the latest improvements than were the company owned tramways of the smaller municipalities.

Some systems never modernised their fleets; a notable example being Bristol whose electric tramway was inaugurated on 14 October 1895 and the first tramcars, when they arrived, were regarded as advanced in every respect and the envy of other towns. Due to a quirk in the Tramways Act of 1870 Bristol Corporation was entitled to take over the company tramway system at book value in 1915, or any seventh year

thereafter; on each occasion the 'seventh year' approached the Corporation vacillated and at the last moment decided to postpone the decision for another seven years, so the company was hardly disposed to invest capital in new or modernised rolling stock. Because of this, the main delivery of tramcars entering service in 1900–1 remained virtually unaltered in appearance and passenger comfort until the system closed down on Good Friday, 11 April 1941 when a German bomb cut St. Philip's bridge in two and severed the main feeder cables.

The basic Bristol tramcar was an open-topped, unbalconied, unvestibuled, four-wheeled double-decker, with four arch-topped windows each side, direct quarter-turn stairs, low dashes and mainly seated 53 passengers. The saloon had single or double bulkhead doors, side-louvre ventilation and longitudinal cushioned bench for 12 passengers

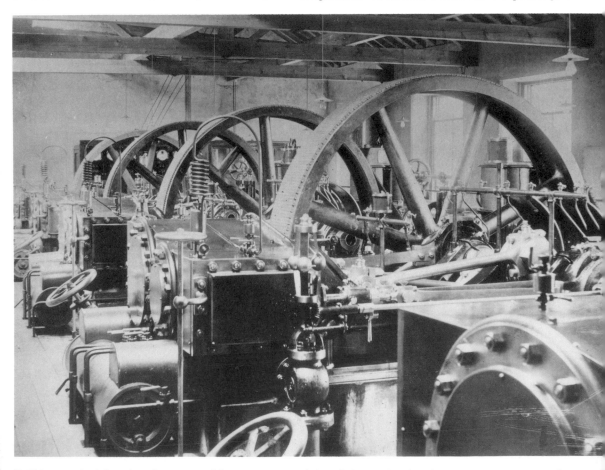

(*left*) Lower deck interior of tramcar with transverse seats. (*London Transport*)

(*above*) An early electric tramway power station with Mather & Platt steam engine driven generators.

each side. The top deck seats in pairs of the reversible 'garden' type, and ventilation was no problem, except that there was too much of it, especially on windy rainy nights!

Another example of the British 'standard' type of tramcar was the Preston built 'Brill' open-topped car with which many systems started and which survived, with various modifications, until quite late in the tramcar era. Also a four-wheeled car, it was similar to the basic Bristol car in all respects except that it was equipped with a full canopy covering the driver, whereas all the Bristol cars had short canopies leaving the driver fully exposed to all the elements. Bristol had 237 cars housed in seven depots sited on various routes in the city. In contrast Gloucester had only 30 electric tramcars and Reading had 36; this gives some indication of the differing requirements of passenger transport in various cities and towns, depending on their populations.

At the beginning of this century electric tramcars were regarded as a prestige symbol by various councils which vied with each other in installing a proliferation of routes within their boundaries without, in some cases, considering the eventual viability from an economic standpoint.

Most electric tramcar liveries reflected the desire of the councillors to make an impression of the distinctive nature of their town and they varied to quite a degree. This was apparent when systems inter-ran and a Salford tramcar running into Manchester reflected that town's individuality as did a green and cream painted car of the company owned Black Country system mingling with Birmingham's municipally owned blue cars.

Tramcar liveries continued in the stage-coach tradition of gay colourings, yellow, cream and red being present in most fleets. Coachbuilding was a craft and the vast majority were craftsmen-built and painted. Some undertakings took such pride in the appearance of their cars that it was not unusual for 12 or more priming, rubbing down and colour

(*below*) Bristol tramcars retained their antiquated design throughout the life of the system, due to a quirk in the tramways Act of 1870 which entitled a local authority to take over the tramways system from a company at seven-year intervals should it so wish. (*Bristol Omnibus Company*)

(*right*) An Ettrick Bay open toastrack electric tramcar with trippers boarding for Rothesay, Isle of Bute. (*The Rev. N. Jackson-Stevens*)

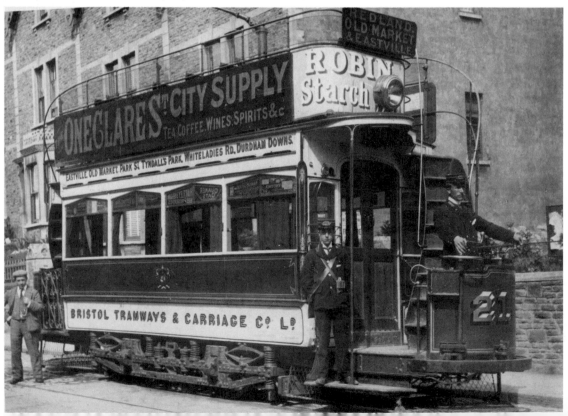

coats of paint and varnish to be applied. Today's passenger carrying vehicles are welded together by mass production methods and spray painted but even a brand new one is not in the same class as one built earlier in this century which still looked immaculate even when it was 20 or 30 years old. The thoroughness and attention to detail of those craftsmen-built cars and which were painted with such care, resulted in reliable vehicles comparatively inexpensive to maintain and service.

It was usual to paint the dashes and the side or waist panels in the same dark colour with the lower, or rocker-panels, the pillars, window-frames and upper deck panels in a lighter colour. All panels were embellished with gold lining and complicated scroll patterns, with the coat of arms of the county, city, local council or owning company on the centre of the waist-panel. It was very rare to see a car with accident-damaged paintwork or a cracked window, unless it was being taken back to a depot for repair, so proud were the various owners of the appearances of their fleets. Compare the coachwork and painting finish of any preserved electric tramcar in those transport museums where they are now to be found, with passenger carrying vehicles now running on our streets.

Interior furnishings and décor also received high-class attention, every possible piece of woodwork was beaded, fluted, bevelled, carved or otherwise ornamented, and window-panes in the

bulkhead doors were bevelled or etched. Seating was of perforated plywood, woven rattan, wooden slats or, occasionally, horsehair filled squabs of fabric. The seats on open-topped cars were generally of wooden slats with a sailcloth or tarpaulin apron to protect the seat when one vacated it in wet weather. Smoking was prohibited on the lower deck and on single-deck cars unless they were divided by a door to isolate the 'smoking compartment' from the 'non-smoking' one. Ladies did not smoke, at least not in public, in the heyday of the tramcar so the upper-deck was a masculine stronghold. It was quite an experience to survive a long journey on the closed top deck of a well filled car in an industrial town with 30 or more workmen's pipes billowing forth the products of the combustion of strong shag and similar pungent asphyxiant mixtures of tobacco. In later years upholstered seats appeared in lower and upper saloons, if the latter were not open-topped ones.

In early days the ceilings of the lower saloons and of the upper saloons of covered-top cars were of decorated mill-board and the woodwork polished or varnished but, latterly, ceilings were painted white, probably to assist the lighting at night. Sliding bulkhead doors were general except at the top of the stairs of enclosed upper-deck saloon cars where the doors were hinged.

Above the lower deck main windows there was usually a series of smaller windows which could be opened for ventilation. The upper decks of covered-top cars sometimes also had similar

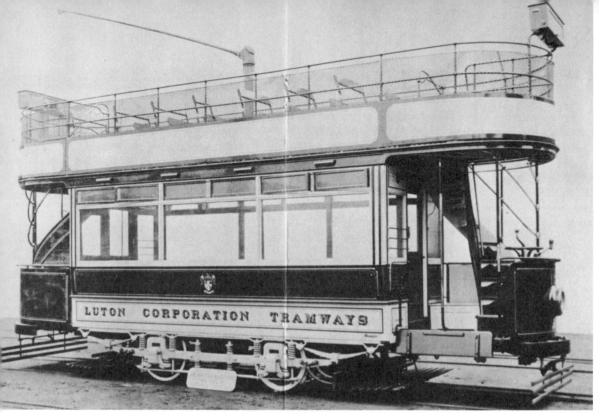

(*above*) Hundreds of this type of open-top four-wheel car were constructed for towns throughout Britain. (*Peter Hammond*)

(*below*) A Croydon Corporation double-deck open top bogie-car with an entirely exposed open platform with no protection whatever for the driver. In severe inclement weather they wore oilskin coats and souwester-type hats. Drivers frequently had their gloves frozen on to the controller and brake handles. (*Geoffrey Baddeley*)

louvre fashion windows but in the main, the windows themselves were made to be lowered.

The first generation of electric tramcars had open platforms but later these were enclosed by glass screens to protect the drivers. The same applied to early covered-top cars; they had open balconies at each end but most were glazed in later days so that the cars were totally enclosed. Transverse seats on both decks were reversible so that one could face the direction of travel.

One curious description of the side-boards protecting the lower part of the upper deck of the

Tramcar drivers were a hardy race able to endure a ten hour tour of duty on open-fronted cars in the early days before glazed vestibules were installed. (*Blackpool Corporation Transport*)

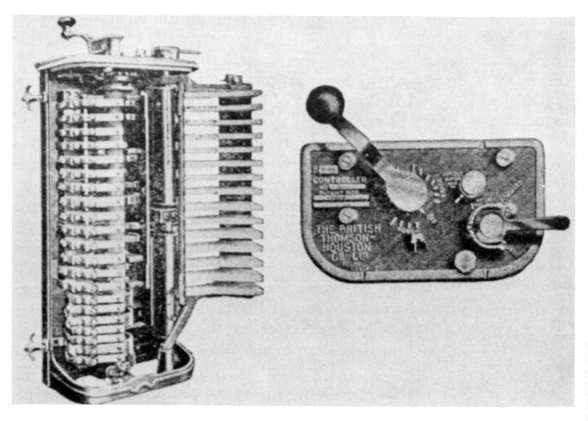

A typical electric tramcar controller showing the interior and the top-plate. The handle on the left controls the speed and the electric brake. The smaller 'key' on the right controls the forward and reverse directions of the car.

open-decked cars seems, in this day and age, quite amusing. These side-panels were always known as 'decency-boards' and were so described on draughtsmen's drawings and stock lists of tramway components. The name derived from the fact that our purist-minded forefathers were *shocked* by the decadent glimpse of a lady's ankle from under the voluminous long skirts of those days when occasionally a lady had ventured to ride on the top deck! Decency-boards were the result and the outside-facing panel was used for advertisements.

Before the days of metal bodies, good hardwoods – oak, beech, ash, teak and mahogany – were used extensively in the framing and panelling. Handrails, guard-rails and stair stringers were of metal as were the dashes; the latter was inherited from horse tram days where it was provided to protect the driver from mud and

filth thrown up by the horses and it was continued into electric days where it protected the driver in the event of a collision. The 'collision-fender' projecting in front of the platform afforded the same protection and it was also used for coupling and towing a disabled car back to the depot.

The platforms at both ends of the car were identical; each had a complete set of controls including the controller and hand brake and in later years, on some cars, the air-brake. Naturally the driver would use the front in whichever direction the car was travelling and the conductor the rear when he was not collecting fares. On double-deck cars the platforms also served as the lower landing for the stairs.

Destination-boxes, illuminated at night, were prominent at both front and rear of the top deck and together with side destination-boards, mounted under the lower windows, showed the terminus and places en route of the tramcar. These were of great assistance to the passenger running to catch the car from any direction, unlike the frustration and confusion caused by present-day passenger vehicles which often have only one indicator, and that at the front.

7

Social Amenities and Cheap Fares

In these days of ever-soaring rail fares, it is difficult to realise that Great Britain once had a cheap, clean, efficient, light-rail system in the majority of its towns which not only had the advantage of not polluting the atmosphere of the streets with pungent diesel and petrol fumes, but provided a very frequent passenger-carrying service for the benefit of all. The main principle of any public transport system is the carriage of passengers in bulk at cheap rates and only by a strict regard for this principle will its existence be justified or its continued success be possible. The last two decades have seen a steady decline in bulk passenger-carrying transport due to a disregard of this vital precept; the proliferation of the ubiquitous motor-car is not the only reason.

Remarkably cheap fares had always been the attraction of electric tramways and in 1902 passengers in Glasgow travelled four stages, approximately $2\frac{1}{4}$ miles, for their 1d. In 1912 London County Council introduced a maximum fare of 3d single, 5d return, anywhere in the county and for this one of the longest rides possible was probably the journey of over 13 miles from Abbey Wood to Victoria Embankment.

In 1920 cheap midday fares from 10am to 4.0pm were introduced whereby the maximum fare was 2d all the way, an astounding transport

The first LCC electric tramcar running to Clapham, 15 May 1903. The Prince of Wales (afterwards King George V) can be seen on the top deck raising his hat in acknowledgement to the welcoming crowds. The car was painted white for the occasion. (*London Transport*)

bargain on the part of London County Council. A lady shopping in, for example, Streatham and not being able to match the material for which she was looking could jump on a car and try other shops in, say, Kennington or the City, for this small sum.

Then in 1925 the LCC launched the one shilling 'All Day Ticket', giving unlimited rides in the county for 24 hours. Some routes even had 'All-night' cars. Later this special ticket was extended to include the East London municipal systems and Croydon Corporation Tramways which had already inaugurated through-running from Purley to the Embankment. The 'All Day Ticket' only cost 6d after 6.0pm for the same unlimited facility. The renowned LCC Tramways Manager was the late Aubrey Llewellyn Coventry Fell, whose oft-quoted dictum, 'I'll make it too dear for you to walk' certainly encouraged travel, as his tramcars were frequently filled to capacity.

Birmingham Corporation at the inauguration for the Whitsun holiday in 1924 of its new modern extension from Selly Oak to the Lickey Hills, which was constructed on segregated 'reserved' track (see page 65) on the median strip of the Bristol Road, charged a fare of 5d for eight miles — from the Navigation Street terminus, centre of Birmingham — and 9d return for the 16 miles. Kinver Light Railway ran a daily excursion car from Birmingham Council House to Kinver, a distance of 18 miles or 36 miles return for 1s 6d. This was a through car but one could book for the same fare and change cars twice on the journey. There were very many more examples of remarkably cheap journeys on most tramway systems in addition to their basic fares which were always a bargain.

As all electric tramway systems provided a very frequent and economical method of transport, it is difficult for the present generation to make any comparison on a cost basis between travelling to shop during that era and present-day shopping. Today the motor car is used even for short journeys and a car-parking fee coupled with the high cost of petrol seems a most expensive way of shopping. Can it be compared with the convenience of the cheap ubiquitous electric

A London tramcar advertising the remarkably cheap fares available whereby passengers could travel all day on 160 miles of tramway changing cars at will for 1s (5p) or 6d (2½p) after 6pm. (*London Transport*)

Birmingham Corporation tramcar in a picturesque tree-lined setting on the Lickey Hill route on the segregated median strip reserved track. (*Birmingham Corporation Transport*)

Birmingham Corporation tramcar No 10 which entered service in January 1904 to operate the first electric tramway route from Steelhouse Lane to Aston Brook Street. Platform vestibules were fitted later, also more powerful motors. They were known as the 'old bogies' and gave 46 years' service until 1950. (*Birmingham Corporation Transport*)

One of the early Glasgow electric four-wheel open top tramcars. Notice the awkward position of the controller behind the stairs. The driver would have to adopt an awkward sideways stance when driving because of the distance between the controller and the handbrake. (*Glasgow Corporation Transport*)

tramcar which was always available every few minutes?

One of the main reasons for the cheapness of fares was that an electric tramcar relied for its power on a central electric generating station, which was very economical producing current on a large scale, and the car, of course, only used this power when it was moving, as is the case with any electric public service vehicle supplied by a generating station. In contrast the present-day bus is equipped with its own power-unit and whether the vehicle is stationary or moving is always burning oil.

There were a number of cases of tramcars being used for funerals, the coffin being placed on a bier inside a car, a window having been removed to gain access, with the cortège of mourners following in other tramcars hired for this purpose. One of the principal 'bulk-hiring' of tramcars came from 'works outings' which were on an annual basis in industrial areas; these works outings were funded by the employees contributing weekly for a year and, usually, topped up by a donation from the firm which organised a fleet of tramcars to convey everyone to some amenable picnic site in the country. Church organisations also engaged fleets of tramcars to take children on Sunday school outings for similar picnics.

In the industrial districts of the Black Country, works outings and Sunday school outings usually ended up either at Kinver – advertised on tramcars as the 'Switzerland of the Midlands' – or the Lickey Hills, near Bromsgrove, another beauty spot well beyond the smoke and noise of the factories. Many other towns took advantage of hiring fleets of tramcars for this and other purposes. Football specials were always available, either hired in fleets or interspersed with normal service cars, to convey football enthusiasts to important matches at reduced fares.

On many systems return Workmen's Fares at exceptionally cheap rates could be purchased before 8.0am, returning on any car after 5.0pm or 6.0pm. How the conductor distinguished between a 'workman' and a clerical employee must have been problematical at times – probably by the absence of a collar and tie in the case of the former.

A few tramway systems had a 'private hire car' equipped with basket-type chairs, small tables and ornately decorated interiors in luxury style. With this high standard of comfort they could be hired for special events such as weddings and theatre-parties.

All British electric tramways were equipped with snow ploughs and not only did they clear the streets for their own vehicles but for other road traffic as well.

8

Typical Leasing Problems in Early Days

The three largest electric tramway systems in Great Britain shared the same difficulties at their inception. In all three cases during the latter part of the last century and the early part of the century, within the environs of London, Birmingham and Glasgow various companies had owned horse or cable-traction tramways. They were operated under lease agreements negotiated with the authorities in whose streets they ran, with, of course, varying terminal dates.

The Tramways Act of 1870 gave power to Local Authorities to purchase their various tramway companies after a period of twenty-one years from the passing of the authorising Acts, with the exception of the original companies who had obtained their initial Acts before the 1870 Tramways Act became law.

Without itemising the labyrinth of legislation entailed in the purchase of the tramways by these three local authorities, it is suffice to record that by 1891 the London County Council was in a position to exercise its rights under the Act on those parts of the horse tramway network which had been in existence since 1870. The extent of the difficulties in Glasgow may be judged by the fact that a volume was published in 1877 containing Acts of Parliament and other documents relative to the various tramways in that city. The whole matter became an issue at the 1890 and 1891 Municipal elections where the voters are said to 'have given a decided expression of opinion in favour of "municipalisation"' resulting in the Corporation deciding to go ahead in creating a tramway system of its own.

On 7 March 1899 Birmingham decided to seek Parliamentary powers to work all the tramways

An early type Metropolitan Electric Tramways car on the Paddington—Sudbury route. (*F. Roche*)

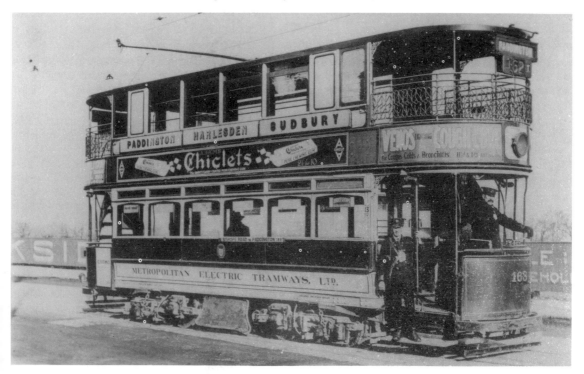

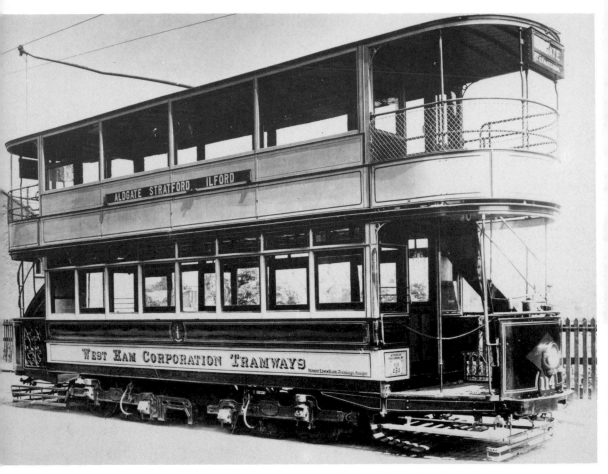

An early type West Ham Corporation electric
tramcar on the Aldgate, Stratford, Ilford route.
(*F. Roche*)

within the city on the expiry of the various leases
and on 9 November 1900 a new Tramways
Committee was formed but it was not until its Act
became law in 1903 that it was empowered to do
so. Meanwhile various other local authorities on
the periphery of the, then, Birmingham
Corporation boundaries had either purchased the
lines within their areas or waived their powers of
purchase and allowed the British Electric Traction
Company to construct tramways within their area.
However plans were afoot for a large extension of
the boundaries of the city but it was not until the
Local Government Board's Provisional Order
(1910) Confirmation (No. 13) Act 1911 that
Birmingham was able to purchase all the tramway
tracks within the enlarged city boundaries.

Electrification of London's tramways was first
considered in 1898 and the method of doing this

delayed its implementation as London County
Council did not favour the idea of its main streets
being festooned with overhead wires. After
examining a conduit-equipped electric car at the
1900 Tramways Exhibition it was decided to
adopt this expensive system of current-collection
for London, with the exception of some outlying
districts, eventually resulting in 123 miles of
conduit track and 43 miles of overhead equipped
track owned or operated by the London County
Council.

The situation in Glasgow was equally
complicated. Unlike Edinburgh, Dundee,
Birmingham and other towns, Glasgow and
London never operated steam tramcars in their
cities but relied on horses, although Birmingham
and Edinburgh did have some cable cars. There
had been constant friction between the Glasgow

34

Westminster Bridge in early days with an LCC open-top car and a recently covered top car. The site of the present County Hall is on the right. The photograph, though, is heavily touched up and the trams appear to have been superimposed on the road scene. (*Greater London Council*)

Tramway and Omnibus Company in the horse-drawn days as there were several complicated issues due to the fact that the Company's routes ran outside the city's boundaries and territories into those of other local authorities. Late in 1891, after an application for the extension of the Company's lease, Glasgow Corporation definitely resolved to 'undertake the working of the tramways as a municipal concern on the expiry of the lease on 30 June 1894'. When the citizens of Glasgow stirred abroad on 1 July 1894 they found the Corporation horse tramway service in complete working order.

After inspecting electric tramway routes in Bristol and Coventry and seeing the headway being made, Glasgow Corporation finally decided to install a demonstration section of electric tramway on its Springburn route in 1898 and the overhead wiring was carried out by their own staff. The success of this encouraged a rapid change to electric traction and the re-laying of the horse-drawn car rails with heavier section rails for the new electric tramcars was undertaken forthwith, keeping the horse cars running all the time. The laying down of ducts along the routes for the distributing cables, setting up a vast electric system, including a large power station with sub-stations, electrically equipping all the lines, rolling stock and depots, together with building and equipping a factory to build their own cars eventually proceeded apace.

Croydon horse tramways, owned by the Croydon Tramways Company had by 1897 fallen into a bad state of repair. Following discussions on the question of purchase Croydon Council called a public meeting on 21 October 1898 resulting in much agitation both for and against the town buying the system. On 19 June 1899, Croydon Corporation decided to purchase the horse tramway system and lease it to the British Electric Traction Company for 21 years from 26 September 1901. However, the Corporation then decided to terminate the lease and on 1 June 1906 took complete control of the tramways. At a later date, the South Metropolitan Electric Tramways and Lighting Company Limited constructed lines to Crystal Palace, Penge, Mitcham and Tooting which terminated within the Croydon boundary and were subject to the powers vested in the Corporation by the Croydon and District Electric Tramways Acts of 1902 and 1903.

Local authorities were able to hold promoters to ransom and, where they intended to operate themselves instead of leasing, frequently took

A South Metropolitan Electric Tramways car at the
Crystal Palace en route for Croydon. (*F. Roche*)

decisions which made through running impossible.
A particularly bad example was in the West Riding
of Yorkshire where the 11 miles from Bradford to
Huddersfield was served by three undertakings.
Bradford had six miles on 4ft gauge, Halifax one
mile on 3ft 6in gauge while Huddersfield worked
the remainder on the odd 4ft 7¾in gauge.

There were, of course, exceptions to this myopic
attitude of some councils and councillors in their
leasing and restrictive practices against electric
tramways. One of the best examples was
Manchester which was unique in being the centre
of a large tramway network which comprised over
300 miles of routes. It was a colourful sight to see
the gaudy red, white, and blue cars of Ashton-
under-Lyme Corporation, the sedate maroon and
ivory cars of Oldham Corporation, the plum and
primrose liveried cars of Rochdale Corporation
and the clumsily-named 'Stalybridge, Hyde,
Mossley and Dunkinfield Tramways and
Electricity Board' green and cream trams mingling
with Manchester's own cars through the main
shopping streets. At the bottom of Market Street
could also be seen the cars of Salford Corporation,
the South Lancashire Tramways Company and, at

one time, those of Bury Corporation. Nowhere
else in the country could the cars of so many
different and independent tramway operators be
seen running on the same tracks. The leasing
problems and complicated financial arrangements
connected with interchange-ticket fares and usage
of each other's electricity supply over various
sections of the many routes covered were not
inconsiderable but the unique public transport
service provided to the travelling public amply
justified them.

In some cases leasing problems were covered by
'balance of mileage' workings, one notable
example concerned the company-owned routes
outside the Birmingham city boundaries. The
company-owned Bearwood line together with the
short length of company-owned track of the Soho
line beyond the Heath Street boundary, were
worked by through Birmingham Corporation
tramcars from the city; these balanced the services
to Dudley from Birmingham permitted to be
operated by the company which also ran some
through services to their Kinver Light Railway in
the summer season.

9

London's Tramways

Local authority boundaries formed artificial barriers on many of the natural traffic flows radiating from London. On a journey from Aldgate to Barking, for example, one passed through no less than four of these – the London County Council, West Ham, East Ham and Barking. In West London similar difficulties were encountered by the London United Tramways Limited. When they applied for powers to construct tramways they discovered that, amongst others, Ealing Council, Wimbledon Council and Kingston Council had joined in a welter of schemes to construct their own tramways.

The year 1900 ended with Bills in hand from Richmond Council and Wimbledon Council to construct and work tramways within their areas. An all-embracing Bill by the London United Electric Tramways designed to smother opposition over a vast area not surprisingly lost many of its provisions at the hands of Parliament. Another Bill was promoted in 1902 by this company but again several lines were disallowed and two were withdrawn by the company due to the excessive demands of the local authorities concerned.

The electric tramways system operated by the Metropolitan Electric Tramways Limited was the largest of the three company-owned tramways in London having a total route mileage of $53\frac{1}{2}$. From the Middlesex County Council they leased $42\frac{1}{2}$ miles just under two from the Hertfordshire

Metropolitan Electric Tramways early type open-top car at East Finchley. (*F. Roche*)

(*above*) Finchley Depot of Metropolitan Electric Tramways. (*F. Roche*)

(*below*) A London United Electric Tramways car passing an overhead repair tower wagon. (*F. Roche*)

(*above*) West Ham Corporation tramcar on the Stratford route. (*F. Roche*)

(*below*) The first LCC electric tramcar across Blackfriars Bridge, London, 14 September 1909, driven by the Lord Mayor, with all the confident aplomb of a civic dignitary quite oblivious that he is operating the controller with the wrong hand! On this type of car the left hand operates the controller, the right hand the handbrake! (*London Transport*)

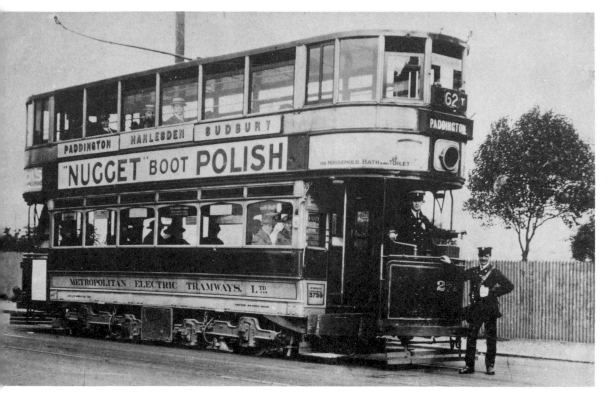

Metropolitan Electric Tramways bogie-tramcar bound for Paddington. (*F. Roche*)

County Council and in addition it operated the services over the London County Council's line from Paddington to Kensal Green. There were also large scale reciprocal arrangements with London County Council whereby Metropolitan cars reached all the northern termini in Central London west of Moorgate.

The South Metropolitan Electric Tramways and Lighting Company Limited, by far the smallest of the company-owned electric tramways, operated routes from West Croydon to Penge, Crystal Palace, Sutton and Mitcham, including Croydon Corporation's branch to Selhurst; its total route mileage was 13.08 miles.

Apart from the company-owned electric tramways in London, the municipally-owned systems comprised the County Borough of Croydon, with a track mileage of 9.28 miles, and the three other small municipal operators of Erith, Bexley and Dartford in the extreme south-east of the metropolis. Walthamstow Corporation's progressive system was inaugurated on 3 June 1905 with lines from Leyton to Woodford, Chingford Mount, Higham Hill and Ferry Lane

with a total of 8.93 route miles and, finally, 62 cars. The Borough of Leyton's system was electrified on 1 December 1906 but on 1 July 1921 was handed over to the London County Council. Barking Borough Council's tramway was electrified on 1 December 1903 and operated until 1929 when taken over by buses.

The County Borough of West Ham opened its first electric line between Stratford, Plaistow and the Abbey Arms on 27 February 1904 and this busy system served a densely populated industrial and dockland area operating a route mileage of 16.27 miles. An early participant in the electric tramway field, East Ham Borough Council began operation on 22 June 1901 along the Barking and Romford roads and between Manor Park Broadway and Beckton Road. Although this council only owned 8.34 miles of track, through running undertaken with the London County Council between Aldgate and Barking increased this mileage considerably. Noted as being the first operator to introduce covered top deck cars to London, Ilford Urban District Council began operation with electric cars in March 1903

An LCC class HR/2 tramcar with equal-traction wheels. This type of car was used on hilly routes and was equipped with four motors of 35hp each for greater adhesion. (*Greater London Council*)

between Ilford and Barking, and Chadwell Heath, inaugurating its service with six open-topped double-deck cars.

By far the largest and best-known electric tramway in the metropolis was the London County Council's own system which at its maximum owned approximately 1,800 cars, operated 167.18 route miles, including the Leyton system which it worked from 1921. Through running was also undertaken on several other systems and London County Council cars could be seen at points as far apart as Barnet, Wimbledon, Purley and Barking.

It would be fair to say that a large majority of London's electric tramcars were bogie-cars with enclosed top-decks and in later years, enclosed platforms to protect the drivers. There were, however, some four-wheel and some single-deck types, the latter mainly for use in the Kingsway Subway before it was heightened to take double-deck cars in 1931, and for service on the Alexandra Palace routes.

Electrification of the vast London County Council system was first discussed in 1898 but due to delays through debating the relative merits of the conduit track, which was finally adopted for the majority of the system, it was not until May 1903 that the first electric lines were inaugurated by the Prince of Wales (later King George V) who drove the inaugural car for part of its journey to Tooting.

Three very short sections of line were within the City of London boundaries and these were built by the City of London Corporation and leased to and maintained by the London County Council.

Of the total route mileage of London County Council's electric tramways 123.30 miles were of conduit track and 43.88 miles overhead trolley-wire; the figures represent mostly double track as there was very little single. Odd numbers were used for routes north of the river Thames and even route numbers to the south, the only exceptions being the services using the Kingsway subway which had route numbers 31, 33 and 35. They provided a fast and frequent connection between various parts of North and South London.

London's conduit current-collection system was very expensive. The renewal in 1927 of the five-way intersection at Aldgate was one of the largest engineering projects ever tackled. (*Greater London Council*)

Great Britain had always been the home of double-deck tramcars in the horse-drawn and steam tramway era so also in the electric era double-deck cars were mainly confined to Great Britain and its Empire. Top-covers had been used on steam car trailers merely to protect passengers from soot and smuts from the tram-engines so the early electric double-deck cars were open-topped. But soon, because of the British climate, the advantages of top-covers became apparent and many existing cars were fitted with them and the new ones being so equipped at assembly. At first the open balcony type was fitted but it was not long before it was replaced by the totally enclosed top-cover.

The regulations of the Metropolitan Police

authority which licensed all London's cars individually, bore heavily upon the design of the cars. The 'reversed staircase' which obstructed the view of the driver to his left-hand side was condemned in early days. Although many tramways used vestibuled screens for the protection of their drivers, in London the Metropolitan Police forbade both tram and bus drivers to have windscreens; this ban lasted until 1931 despite frequent appeals by all the tramway undertakings to have it lifted.

London's tramways operated fleets of well-tried traditional equipment relying on superb maintenance to give the maximum efficiency. By 1903 most of the problems in electric tramway operation had been overcome and almost all

A plough change-pit in Mile End Road, London, looking east. The outward-bound cars shed their ploughs at these change-pits, proceeding to the terminus on the overhead trolley-wire system. The ploughs were guided through the conduit junction and held ready for city-bound cars using the conduit system when these cars took on the ploughs. The 'ploughman' can be seen guiding the plough with his fork into the plough-channels of the a city-bound car. (*London Transport*)

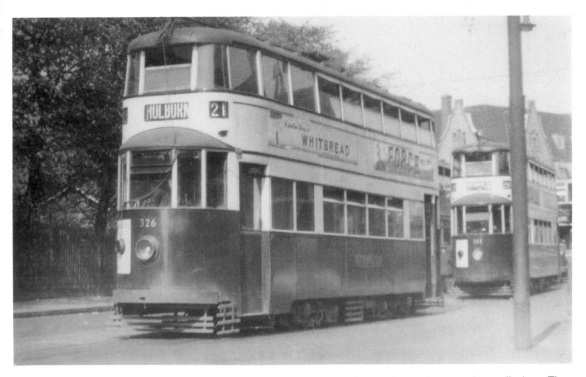

Two of the renowned London 'Feltham' cars in their Metropolitan Electric Tramways days. The 'Felthams' were of the double-saloon type, all-enclosed, of all metal construction, with special driving-cabs and spacious end vestibules. They weighed 18 tons 6cwt unloaded and were equipped with two 70hp motors.

(*above*) Another 'Feltham' car on 'All Night' service at Tooting Broadway. The 'All Night' trams provided a reliable and efficient half-hourly service throughout the night, mainly used by newspaper and railway staffs, bakers, nurses and other shift workers. (*London Transport*)

(*below*) Flooded roadways did not always deter tramcars from getting their passengers to their destinations. Another two 'Felthams' in North London, nearly waterborne. (*Fox Photos*)

A busy scene at Victoria Station, London, in 1932 with two LCC cars besieged by eager passengers boarding the tramcars by both platforms. Most London tramcars were dual-equipped for overhead and conduit current collection but the front car is equipped for conduit track only as its roof has no trolley pole. (*Greater London Council*)

London's tramcars used equipment which had been perfected under service conditions for several years. The conduit system pioneered in Blackpool in 1885 had been widely applied in the USA and parts of Europe and the more generally-used overhead trolley-wire system had been brought to a high level of performance.

The same basic design in the main remained standard until the abandonment of the electric tramways in the early 1950s, with the exception of a new and revolutionary designed tramcar which, after some trials with experimental models, made its appearance on the Metropolitan Electric Tramways and the London United Electric Tramways in 1931. Known as the 'Feltham', because it was built by the Union Construction and Finance Company Limited at Feltham in Middlesex, 46 were supplied to the London United and the remainder, 54, to the Metropolitan Electric Tramways.

The Felthams combined the best and most advantageous features of the three experimental cars. The same basic lines were apparent including the rear entrance and front exit layout to facilitate quick loading and unloading, protruding driver's cabs and an overall length of 40ft making it the longest passenger carrying vehicle running on the streets of London at that time. There was provision for seating a total of 64 passengers, some 10 fewer than the standard London tramcars, but the vestibules provided ample room for a further 10 standing at each end, making the maximum capacity 84. The main endeavour had been to provide the greatest comfort for passengers in normal traffic combined with a large 'rush-hour' capacity and in this the Felthams were successful.

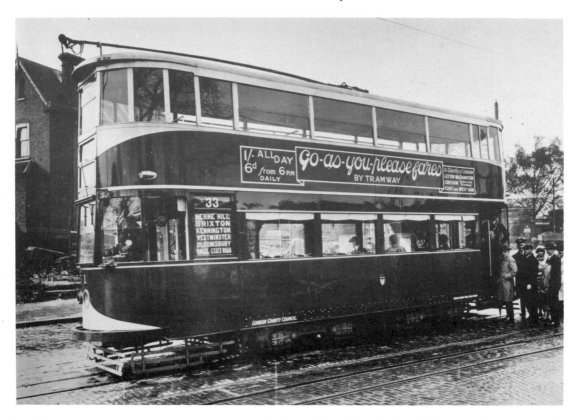

The LCC's answer to the company-owned 'Feltham' cars. This LCC car was constructed at its Charlton works in 1932, the prototype of what was intended to be a fleet of luxury tramcars. Known as the 'blue car' it was in blue livery and distinguished by the luxury of its appointments. The motorman had a fully-enclosed cab and the car being numbered was said to presage a new fleet of 500 similar ca which, due to a change of policy when Lond Transport took over on 1 July 1933, nev materialised. (*London Transport*)

Their first appearance on 1 February 1931 made a marked impression on the travelling public; a welcome innovation on London's tramcars was that they were fitted with heaters. Interior bulkheads had been dispensed with and the seat coverings and decor of both saloons were of an exceptionally high standard. Because of a combination of fast loading and unloading, together with rapid acceleration and deceleration, the latter due to particularly efficient air braking, the Felthams were able to maintain an average service speed of 12mph including stops, the highest obtained on any urban tramway in the country. This notable achievement has remained a record. They were also equipped with two 70hp motors attaining a 20mph acceleration in 20 seconds.

After the abandonment of electric tramways in the Metropolitan and London United areas of

London, the Felthams were transferred to Sou London in 1936 where they gave splendid serv until the termination of London's tramways. T remaining 89, those which had survived the 'bli of the second world war, London Transport so to Leeds and they continued in service there un the closure of the tramways in 1959. One Feltha survives today and can be seen in the Lond Regional Transport Museum at Covent Gard having been presented to it by enthusiasts who h restored it to its former Metropolitan Elect Tramways livery and fleet number, 355.

(*right*) The upper saloon of LCC car No 1, the only c of its type, shows the high standard of luxu attained. (*London Transport*)

Trailers were put into operation by the LCC on 7 June 1913 and were used on a few routes. They were a boon during the 1914–18 war but when newer higher-powered cars were delivered after the war it was revealed that these cars, operating singly, could provide a far superior service and the trailers were withdrawn on 17 April 1924. (*London Transport*)

10
Some Urban Systems

During the early 1920s there were approximately 180 electric tramway services operating in the towns of Great Britain, 101 of which were municipally-owned and 79 company-owned. In some towns electric tramcars were introduced and initially operated by companies before being taken over by the municipal authorities, also some municipal authorities owned the lines in their areas and allowed them to be operated by companies while, later on, other systems merged and were re-titled.

In 1929 Manchester was operating more than 950 tramcars over its 123 miles of track, Birmingham finally owned 843 cars, and Liverpool operated 788 cars over 97 route miles, Glasgow's fleet attained 1,100 cars while Newcastle-upon-Tyne's fleet was more than 300 strong. At the lower end of the scale came Taunton, a company-owned tramway which operated 1.66 miles of track with only six cars and the Swansea & Mumbles electric line with, eventually, 13 very modern double-deck cars seating 106 passengers, the largest cars in the country.

Sheffield Corporation received Parliamentary powers to operate its tramways and to use electric power; it took over from the previous company when its lease terminated on 10 July 1896, acquiring 44 tramcars, 310 horses and nine miles of track. It lost no time in converting all lines to electric traction, re-laying the tracks with heavier rails for the electric cars and extending outwards from the city centre. Under the able guidance of the new electrical engineer Aubrey Llewellyn Coventry Fell, later General Manager of London County Council tramways, the first electric car ran on 5 September 1899 heralding a fare reduction from 2d to 1d all the way from the city to the various termini, with $\frac{1}{2}$d fare stages. Although using a few single-deck cars on routes with low railway bridges, Sheffield's fleet consisted mainly of double-deck cars of a very modern design in blue and cream livery. These colours in varying proportions continued to be used on its fleet of 468 electric tramcars during the whole 60 years of operation. Sheffield only used four-wheel cars of

A large Manchester Corporation tramway depot.

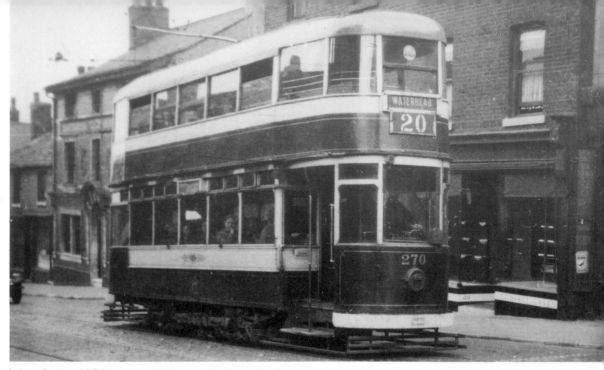

(*above*) In 1930 some high-speed four-wheel 'Pilcher' cars (so called after the then General Manager) were introduced by Manchester Corporation with two 50hp motors, upholstered seats throughout and deep domed roofs painted silver, constructed at its Hyde Road works.

(*below*) A Sheffield tramcar, one of 36 built in 1950–52. All Sheffield cars were capacious four-wheel double-deckers with some of the lowest fares in Great Britain. Car No 502 is shown at Beauchief. (*Charles Roberts & Co Ltd*)

Two Leeds tramcars on the 'reserved' track at Middleton: four-wheel car on the left and one of the 'Felthams' purchased from London when that system finished in 1952.

quite large capacity and never operated any bogie-cars.

Leeds conducted experiments with the first overhead trolley-wire operated electric tramway in England on Graff Baker's Roundhay Park route of about two miles of track in 1891, the tramcars having two 15hp motors. Trouble quickly ensued as the telephone company was using an earth return for its telephone lines and when the tramway did the same for its traction current the result was disastrous. A court injunction stopped the tramway from using an earth return and delay occurred while the learned judge decided that the earth was for anyone to use! The telephone company then installed an insulated return. After those first unfortunate trials the route was temporarily taken over by steam traction but Leeds was actually the first municipality to operate its own electric cars when the Kirkstall to Roundhay service was opened on 2 August 1897. Many interesting cars were used in Leeds, both bogies and four-wheel types; in the final years of operation, Leeds purchased a variety of tramcars from other systems, including the entire remaining fleet of London's Feltham cars. It also had extensive reserved track sections of route on which fast speeds were attained with a fleet of double-deck cars.

Edinburgh retained some of its cable-cars until 1920–3, the last in Great Britain to be electrified. The cable system employed a cable running continuously in a conduit beneath the tracks which could be picked up or released by a 'gripper' with metal jaws suspended from under the car and passing through a slot in the road to reach the cable and operated by a wheel or lever by the driver. Powerful wheel-brakes were fitted to the cars and, in addition, some had slipper track-brakes. The Edinburgh cable system was the fourth largest cable-operated tramway in the world; in 1903 there were some 205 eight-wheel double-deck cars on about 36 miles of route. Edinburgh was late in the electric field, about 20 years later than most so it had a very up-to-date and modern electric system which, at its zenith comprised 360 cars, all double-deck covered-top four-wheel vehicles, on 48 miles of track. Many of the fleet had all-metal bodywork and the Edinburgh livery was a sombre dark brown.

Liverpool's electrification commenced in 1897 when the Corporation purchased 30 German cars built by Busch of Hamburg to replace its horse-drawn tramcars and in 1898–9 followed this with the purchase of 15 American centre-entrance single-deck cars of which some were later converted as double-deckers. Various reasons have been given for some undertakings purchasing

electric tramcars from abroad during this period but the main reason that British tramcar builders were overwhelmed with orders is probably correct. Liverpool experimented with several innovations to its four-wheel and eight-wheel fleet including short top-covers on its double-deck tramcars, leaving the balconies exposed and in early days it tried trailer-cars for a short period; another was with a few 'first class' cars with 'first class fares', these cars, painted white to distinguish them from the rest of the fleet, lasted from 1911 until 1923 before they were withdrawn. With 97 route miles and 788 cars Liverpool also distinguished itself in the electric tramway era by constructing advanced streamline-type cars in 1936/7 to add to its fleet, both bogie-type and four-wheel cars. Out of its 97 route miles of tramway. Liverpool had more 28 miles of reserved track, more than any other British city: it was segregated on the median-strip

An Edinburgh Corporation tramcar in Princes Street, Edinburgh, a city which was late in the electrification field, retaining some of its cable tramcars as late as 1923. It had a very modern electric system and all cars were double-deck four-wheelers with covered-top.

51

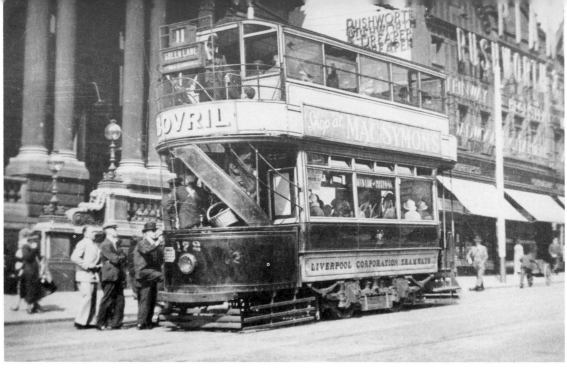

The first Liverpool cars to receive top covers were equipped with what was known as the 'Bellamy' roof which extended only over the centre section and left the balconies uncanopied. (*R. B. Parr*)

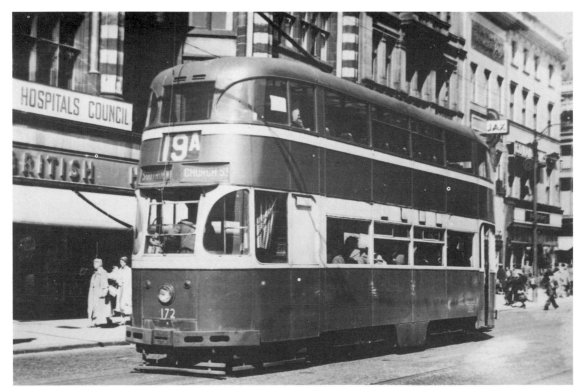

An advanced design streamlined Liverpool totally-enclosed double-deck bogie-car which ran on reserved tracks in addition to city routes. Between 1936–39 Liverpool bought or built 362 very modern cars and opened 10 new route extensions.

Belfast Corporation took over its former horse-drawn tramway in 1905 and electrified all routes. The illustration is of an early-type open top double-deck car. (*W. J. Haynes*)

which divided the dual carriageway, and the well-maintained sleeper track enabled exceptionally high speeds to be attained, the trams frequently overtaking private motor cars.

Belfast tramways commenced with horse-drawn trams in 1872, owned by the Belfast Street Tramways Company until 1 January 1905 when Belfast Corporation took them over and electrified all the routes. Unusually, Belfast track was to a gauge of 5ft 3in, but not surprisingly since it was the same as the Irish railways. Although most of the routes were comparatively short, in many cases only two miles long, the traffic, in the mammoth shipbuilding yards area was most intense. One route, Queens Road, during the rush hour in which the tramcars were nose-to-tail

taking shipyard workers home to the suburbs has been described as more heavily-trafficked than Westminster Embankment in London. The 52 electrified route-miles were served by 441 cars, 50 being replacements built in 1932 and another 50, of an advanced 'Pullman' modern type, made their appearance in 1935; yet this system was replaced by trolleybuses and motor buses between 1944 and 1954, giving a very short life in many cases to this excellent tramway fleet.

Unlike other British networks in large cities, Birmingham had the unique distinction of being operated on a 3ft 6in track gauge, a relic of the horse-drawn and steam tramway days. Despite the restrictions imposed by the limitations of so narrow a gauge, visiting engineers and tramway

(*above*) A Birmingham bogie-car on a reserved track section. All Birmingham cars were of a standard design but they were immaculately maintained and, although the gauge was 3ft 6in, they attained high speeds, particularly on segregated sections of the system. (*Maley & Taunton*)

(*below*) The last tramcar built for Birmingham, in 1930. It was a lightweight experimental car with a deeply domed roof and weighed 12 tons 6cwt, 4 tons 9cwt lighter than a standard Birmingham bogie-car. It is shown at Pebble Mill Road; the tramway clock was operated by motormen to 'clock-in' the arrival of cars at this point. (*R. T. Coxon*)

students from abroad were constantly fascinated to find double-deck Birmingham cars weighing 17 tons giving such a splendid and efficient service. Although the Birmingham car was thought, in some quarters, to be somewhat old-fashioned in appearance it has to be borne in mind that on its introduction each class of car was considered to be the most up-to-date of its kind in the country, embodying many new features which after due testing were considered necessary or advantageous. The standard of design compared well with that of other cities because of the constant development, reconditioning and re-equipping of older cars until as late as 1950, only two years before abandonment. During the electric tramway era Birmingham citizens enjoyed a service which was second to none with cars always remarkably immaculate in their blue livery and the Kyotts Lake Road Repair Works always giving a

high standard of maintenance. The rapid expansion of the city demanded a high degree of rolling stock utilisation, together with a large addition of cars which brought the total in service to a final 825 operating over approximately 150 miles of route, with extremely cheap fares.

Contemporary accounts give the best impression of the importance of the innovation to electric tramways in Glasgow. 'When the first electric tramcars ran from Mitchell Street to Springburn crowds assembled and gazed with open mouth in amazement and admiration at the swift moving vehicles gliding along under the command of some strange unseen force'. The electric tramcars were described as clean and noiseless adding that 'a pace can be attained which the horse tram could never attempt and the excellence of the brakes makes this pace less and less a source of danger'. Possibly the most

Bradford's extensive system was operated mainly by four-wheel covered-top double-deck cars, and some routes were on reserved track sections.
(*W. J. Haynes*)

Glasgow designed an entirely new streamlined tramcar incorporating many new and interesting features. Built at its Coptlawhill works between 1948 and 1952, a hundred of these 'Cunarder' bogie-type tramcars, strikingly impressive in their gleaming dominant orange livery, were most efficient and speedy. (*Glasgow Corporation Transport*)

important single factor in making the tramcars an integral part of the Glasgow man's life was the halfpenny fare. This was introduced by the Corporation when it took over the tramway service, partly to attract new passengers but also to counter the horse bus company's attempt to put more rival buses into service. The innovation was so popular that 40 per cent of all tickets sold in the opening months were halfpenny tickets. It was so cheap that people hopped on and off tramcars for very short distances.

The successful inauguration of electric traction on the Mitchell Street – Springburn route with 21 single-deck cars on 13 October 1898 encouraged the Corporation to take the plunge on 5 January 1899 with its decision to electrify by the overhead trolley-wire system with 'as much progress as possible made before the opening of the International Exhibition in May 1901'. However,

all was ready for the official opening by the Lord Provost on 24 April 1901, a week before the exhibition opened. The single-deck cars were phased out when the new works were established at Coptlawhill and it constructed double-deck cars. The original halfpenny fare was superseded by the 'two stage halfpenny fare' in 1911 with corresponding 2d, $2\frac{1}{4}$d and 3d and over for fares of longer distances. Of 95 miles of double-track in 1909 about 38 miles were not in Glasgow which in Edwardian days did not include Govan, Partick, Pollokshaws and Rutherglen; unlike most English cities, Glasgow Corporation owned, instead of leasing, those lines outside its boundaries, some of which were afterwards incorporated into the enlarged city area. The Corporation also owned tramways in Milngavie, Clydebank and Renfrew with extensive sections in the counties of Lanark, Renfrew and Dunbarton; all these were in addition to the lines of the Airdrie and Paisley companies which it eventually took over. Its electric fleet reached a maximum of 1,208 cars by 1948 with a maximum of 135 miles of double-track; 200 of its tramcars were over 50 years old at the time of abandonment in 1962.

The neighbouring cities of Manchester and Salford operated many tramway routes with a lot of through running by top-covered bogie-cars in identical liveries. At its zenith Manchester had the third largest tramway system in Britain with 950 cars and its 123 miles of route only being exceeded by London County Council and Glasgow. Salford's additional 230 cars and another 40 miles of track made this dual-system larger than Glasgow's; additionally Manchester and Salford also operated 14 municipal systems besides their own.

Bristol Tramways & Carriage Company Limited converted its first horse-drawn tramway service to electric traction on 14 October 1895 when it worked the Old Market to St George route with electric power. It was not until 22 December 1900 that the entire local tramway system was electrically operated; this included a new line from Durdham Downs to Cheltenham Road, a so called 'light railway' from Kingswood to Hanham, and some extensions of the old horse tram routes. Bristol trams were open-topped, unbalconied, unvestibuled four-wheel double-deck cars with the top-deck seats of the reversible garden type transversely placed, a design which remained, without any modernisation, throughout the life of Bristol tramways which ended with one of Hitler's bombs destroying the power supply in April 1941. The fleet reached a maximum of 237 cars, identical in type, the largest fleet in Britain without a covered top, always well-maintained but always under the 'seven year purchase threat' which was eventually carried out by Bristol Corporation in 1937 only as a 'sleeping partner' confining its activities to the financial aspect.

11

Tramways of the 'Black Country'

A number of books and bookets have been written and considerable research undertaken on quite a number of electric tramway systems in Great Britain. It is strange that, other than one which was concerned with the minute detail of construction and operation, no overall description of the tramway of that vast combination known as the 'Black Country' exists, particularly as all the multifarious difficulties exemplified in the introduction of electric tramways in Great Britain were encountered in this area of England, typifying the obstructing and bureaucratic unimaginative outlook of local authorities.

The 'Black Country', mainly within the area of a triangle between Birmingham, Wolverhampton and Stourbridge, now known as the West Midlands, was rich in mineral deposits, coal, ironstone and limestone, and with pockets of clay, attracted the attention of industrialists early in the nineteenth century. Although in 1740 the discovery by the Earl of Dudley of manufacturing bar-iron with coal instead of wood was beginning to be exploited and in 1748 the manufacture of brass was established in Birmingham, it was the early nineteenth century that marked the amazing growth of the many towns within this area. It became known as the Black Country because of the forest of tall chimney stacks that belched forth their thick black smoke, polluting and clouding the atmosphere.

With the development of manufacturing industries, mines and iron-works the necessity for travel became apparent and the Birmingham District Tramway Company Limited was formed on 29 July 1871 with powers authorised under the Birmingham & Staffordshire Tramways Act 1870. It was followed by the Staffordshire Tramways Company Limited on 28 November 1878 whose principal objects were the promotion and construction of tramways in the area. The lines could be operated by animal power and, with the consent in writing of the local authority through whose areas they operated, by steam or any mechanical power '. . . during a period of seven years, also, with such consent and that of the Board of Trade, during further periods of seven years'. The regulations under which they were allowed to operate were very stringent indeed, covering the emission of smoke from tram-engines, noise, speed, efficient brakes and scores of other detailed rules.

Following the many vicissitudes of the horse, steam and, in Birmingham, cable tramways, and after experiments with electric accumulator tramcars, the re-formed South Staffordshire Tramways Company decided to explore the possibilities of electric traction using power supplied to the cars by overhead trolley wires. Walsall Town Council had stated early in 1891 that it would not agree to the use of steam-power after December 1892. Then in April 1891 the company was approached by both Walsall and Wednesbury Town Councils with proposals for electrification.

Black Country double-deck car No 43 of the South Staffordshire area in early days at Pleck (Walsall). This was a standard type car until they were replaced by single-deck totally-enclosed cars in the 1920s. (*J. S. Webb*)

(above) The Birmingham & Midland Tramways Joint Committee, responsible for the company-owned system in the Black Country, changed its policy of partly double-deck cars and some single-deck cars to a fleet of mainly single-deck totally-enclosed cars of a very modern design (with the exception of those running into Birmingham) in the early 1920s. These were built by the Brush Electrical Engineering Co, the rest at its Tividale works.

(below) A 1899 scene in Harts Hill depot, Brierley Hill with the first type cars built by the Brush Engineering Co of Loughborough for the Dudley, Stourbridge & District Electric Traction Co.

A very rare photograph illustrating the method of current collection known as the 'surface contact' system, taken at Wolverhampton. The tramcar carried a 'skate' underneath which electro-magnetically attracted the studs, seen between the tracks. Under the roadway was a continuous power cable in contact with the studs. Immediately the skate broke contact with the studs by the passage of the car, they returned to the 'dead' position by the action of a spring, thus becoming de-energised. In later days there were cases of the springs failing to return to the neutral position and horses with steel horse-shoes received an electric shock. The horses were not particularly pleased and eventually all stud contact systems were converted to overhead trolley operation. (*Express & Star, Wolverhampton*)

About this time the company issued a 14 page booklet entitled *Electric Traction for Ordinary Tramways, Descriptive Pamphlet 1891*, which extolled the virtues of the overhead system and concluded by recommending to their shareholders the equipping of the tramway from Bloxwich to Wednesbury via Walsall with this method.

Two pioneers, associated both with the company and with the local authorities concerned, had visited America where electric tramways had been in operation in many cities for some years and, on their return, reported favourably on the possibilities of this form of traction for the Black Country. After demurring at the 'unsightliness' of overhead wires the authorities visited Roundhay Park, Leeds to inspect the first overhead electric tramways system that had been opened in Britain in October 1891. Later the Chairman of the company stated at an Extraordinary General Meeting that 'he was very glad to tell them that the authorities had unanimously consented to the introduction of electric tramways in the district without a single dissentient voice'.

Work proceeded apace and the existing steam tramway depots at Darlaston and Birchills, near Bloxwich were converted for electric traction. A generating station was built at Walsall, near a canal from which coal could be delivered, equipped with three Lancashire boilers, each having a working pressure of 120lb/sq in, powering three horizontal-coupled compound engines, each of 125hp at 100revs per minutes, and each driving by multiple-cotton ropes at 450revs per minute a direct current dynamo with an output of 260 amps at 350 volts. The normal line-voltage was 300, a low voltage by subsequent standards as electric tramways usually operated on a line-voltage of 550/600 volts dc.

The rolling-stock for these electrified lines consisted of 16 short double-deck four-wheel cars with short canopies and horse-car type staircases at each end; there was seating for 18 inside and 22 outside passengers in an overall length of only 22ft and a weight of only 6 tons 13cwt. Two 15hp motors were installed with the controllers mounted in what must have been a most awkward operating position under the stairs at each end.

The opening ceremony took place on 31 December 1892 in the presence of the Lord Bishop of Lichfield, the Mayors of Walsall, Wednesbury, and West Bromwich, the Chairman and Directors of the Tramway Company and the Chairman and Directors of the Electric Construction

Corporation. The electrified lines were opened to the public next day, 1 January 1893, but steam traction continued to be used on neighbouring lines throughout the Black Country.

The scene changed with the formation of the British Electric Traction Company Limited on 26 October 1896 after the passing of the Light Railways Act of that year. The object of the new company was to develop electric tramways throughout the country, both by promoting and constructing new lines and by obtaining control and reconstructing for electric operation of existing tramways. In addition, when it found that it could not obtain control because the local authorities had purchased or built the lines the BET Company accepted a lease to operate them for a number of years.

In several cases of lines which it controlled the BET Company was the actual operator of the tramways in the early years then after a time the normal method was to form local companies to act as the operators under its control. After several years these particular local companies took over control and operation from the BET.

Thus we have a proliferation of actual operating companies comprising the Birmingham & Midland Tramway Ltd, Birmingham Tramways & Omnibus Co Ltd, City of Birmingham Tramways Co, Dudley Stourbridge & District Electric Traction Co Ltd, Dudley Sedgley & Wolverhampton Tramways Co Ltd, South Staffordshire Tramways Company, South Staffordshire Tramways (Lessee) Co Ltd, and Wolverhampton District Electric Tramways Ltd (which in 1912 became incorporated in the Birmingham & District Power and Traction Co Ltd) with the Birmingham & Midland Tramways Joint Committee co-ordinating and overseeing all aspects of electric tramway operation under its jurisdiction.

The City of Birmingham Tramways Company's last routes had, by the end of 1911 been taken over by Birmingham Corporation, so the Company went into voluntary liquidation and a new company was formed to liquidate the assets. Birmingham & Midland Tramways had had a very large shareholding in the City of Birmingham Company and received a proportionate holding in the new Company.

Here again, one of the BET's principal difficulties was caused by section 43 of the Tramways Act of 1870 whereby a local authority had the option of purchasing any tramways within

A Tramway Parcels Express car drawing a trailer wagon. This was a lucrative side of the Black Country tramways and provided a quick service throughout a wide area, for parcels and even milk churns were conveyed on the Light Railway from the rural village of Kinver.

its district after a lapse of 21 years from their authorisation and thereafter after every seven years, which always made it difficult to induce investors to supply the necessary cash for improvements.

Between 1897 and 1902 the BET advanced proposals for the purchase of all tramways in the district and the electrification and extension on a uniform 3ft 6in gauge system, to be followed by negotiations with all local authorities concerned to delay compulsory purchase or to grant leases to their companies for a minimum of 21 years duration. Walsall and Wolverhampton decided to purchase and operate their respective tramways themselves, but agreements were reached with all other authorities in the areas outside Birmingham.

In the main, the consolidation of the electric tramways in the Black Country into one unified system for operation purposes seemed to be assured by these proposals. In practice, however, the ownership of the lines in a number of towns, after converting them with heavier rail to take the new electric cars, was acquired by some of them, notably Dudley, Smethwick, West Bromwich and Handsworth, and were then leased to the Company to operate. Additionally Dudley Corporation insisted that electric current should be purchased by the Company from the Corporation's own power station and supplied to all lines running within the Borough boundary.

Sometimes curious anomalies occurred, because of local peculiarities. In at least one street in the Black Country the local authority owned the track on one side of the street while the Company owned it on the other side, the boundary running down the middle of the road! Also, in the case of Wolverhampton, no trolley-wires existed as their tramcars used the Lorrain stud-contact system, so when through running was finally agreed a number of the cars had to be dual-equipped to collect current from both systems.

As the Birmingham & Midland Tramways Joint Committee, since its formation in 1904, had been operating the whole tramways system throughout the Black Country owned by the four companies, the major rolling stock redistribution, which resulted from the large batch of cars displaced after the Birmingham Corporation took over the City of Birmingham Tramway Company's system, completed in 1912, meant that quite a number of these cars became available for operating lines in the areas worked by the four subsidiary companies of the BET.

A variety of interesting types of rolling stock was used due to the difficult terrain of the Black Country with its steep hills, very narrow roads and, in some districts, the constant problem of frequent and serious mining subsidences, particularly in South Staffordshire, resulting in substantial packing and renewing the foundations of the track and also in restoring traction-poles to their vertical positions. Added to this were a few very low railway bridges where only single-deck cars could be used; on one main route the Board of Trade prohibited the use of covered-top double-deck cars and some years later also forbade even the use of open-top cars.

In consequence, the fleets of the four operating companies varied from double-deck four-wheel covered-top cars to open-top bogie and four-wheel cars and from single-deck bogie to four-wheel cars, each being used according to the area and traffic conditions to which they were suited.

In early days there were no loading restrictions so most of the fleets were subjected to heavy overloading which resulting in shortening the life of the vehicles. The overloading was accentuated by the acute shortage of staff during the first world war when the cars had to carry huge loads of munition workers in addition to ordinary passengers. One local councillor complained to his council that he had counted 71 passengers on a single-deck four-wheel car designed to carry 28 seated people! Another source of drastic overloading was evident on dark nights when it was pouring with rain and as the lower deck of the car became full with no room for more standing passengers the conductor would call out 'On top only!' indicating that some seats were available there. Unfortunately in the surge forward the conductor frequently could not keep accurate count of the passengers ascending the stairs. No standing was allowed on the top deck but, conversely, in severely inclement weather passengers could not sit on wet seats, so the conductor on making up his way bill, would often discover that he had issued 90 plus tickets on a 54 seater car! This was by no means unusual and although the companies did not mind this extra revenue the overloading took its toll on the cars. Under these conditions, the fleets, after only 20 years of service, had to be replaced and a policy of single-deck vehicles of an advanced design was inaugurated. To grasp the significance of this chronic overloading and its eventual repercussion, it is necessary to realise that Glasgow was using in its fleet some 200 cars which were more than 50 years old at closure in 1962!

12

The Tramcar Supreme — Reserved Track Expansions

The possibilities of light railway construction using electric tramcars on segregated private rights-of-way which could also be operated on street-paved sections of the system were first exploited by the British Electric Traction Company in the early part of this century. The Kinver Light Railway was opened to traffic on 5 April 1901, a Good Friday, and the line carried very heavy traffic on that day and the ensuing Bank holiday to such an extent that the promoters were caught unawares. The same happened at Whitsuntide, the traffic being described an 'enormous' and by mid-afternoon on the Monday an increased service had to be put on using three extra cars which had been recently delivered — all single-deck bogie-cars which were the type mainly used on this line.

The only possible explanation for this overwhelming influx of day trippers to Kinver was the attraction of the pure air and amenities of the countryside compared with the dingy smoke-laden towns. The Kinver Light Railway offered the populace an exciting five mile journey from

A Kinver scene on the Light Railway in early days. These cars, built in 1901 by the Brush Electrical Engineering Co of Loughborough for the 3ft 6in gauge on maximum-traction bogies, were later equipped with glazed windows, and electric headlights were installed in the centre of the dashes. This type of open toastrack car was restricted to summer use, spending the winters in a depot on the Light Railway near Kinver, described as the most rural and isolated tramway depot in the country.

A Kinver Light Railway single-deck later-type bogie-car adaptable for summer and winter use, seen at Kinver terminus. These cars were built at the company's Tividale works in 1915. The milk churns in the picture await the arrival of the Tramway Parcels Express although occasionally they were conveyed on passenger cars.

Stourbridge for the cost of only 3d to the renowned 'Kinver Edge' from which an extensive view of Shropshire was possible; many people saw for the first time broad luscious pastures, an abundance of fine trees and wonderful wild scenes.

This Light Railway, the first of its type in England, ran on street-track for the first mile or so and then forsook the roadway and moved over to a line on a side pathway laid on sleeper-track to the Black Country gauge of 3ft 6in. It continued on sleeper-track to the junction of the Wolverhampton – Kidderminster and Bridgnorth – Birmingham roads where it ran on paved street-track for a short distance. It then entered the fields again on to sleeper-track where it remained within its own fenced right-of-way through a variety of lovely scenery, wooded in places, and along the tree-sheltered river and canal to Kinver terminus.

Another innovation of this pioneer Light Railway was that on the sleeper section of the line all the traction poles were of timber, similar to telegraph poles, and the cost was only £27,167 plus the cost of a generating station. It was extraordinary that this remarkably cheap method

of light railway construction was not adopted more extensively in Britain. It had been widely used in America and on the continent of Europe but it was quite a number of years before electric tramway undertakings woke up to the unique possibilities of this 'reserved' or 'segregated' track on its own right-of-way.

The Burton & Ashby Light Railway, also 3ft 6in gauge, used exclusively by open-top four-wheel cars owned by the Midland Railway, provided another early example of sleeper-track for part of its 10 mile route from Burton through various villages to Ashby. Constructed in 1906 it was built as an alternative to a costly full size railway.

Many years later Liverpool became the ultimate in light railway segregated-track with the longest in Britain, 28 miles out of its total of 97 route miles. It made full use of the construction of sleeper-track on the median-strip which divided the dual carriageways. This segregated-track together with the modernisation programme of its rolling-stock from 1933 and later its advanced fast streamliners in 1936–7 made the journey from the city homewards considerably quicker than in most other cities lacking in this enterprise.

Birmingham, however, had not been slow to grasp the possibilities of sleeper-track on the median-strips around Birmingham. Probably the best known was the route from Navigation Street right out to the Lickey Hills, Rednal, a distance of eight miles for a fare of 5d! The extension from

(*above*) Bristol Road, Birmingham showing bogie-car No 841 on the central reservation median strip which divides the dual-carriageway. (*K. G. Harvie*)

(*below*) One of the 'Middleton' bogie cars which ran from Leeds to Middleton forsaking the streets at Moor Lane a short distance from the city centre and taking a very picturesque course on sleeper track through Middleton Woods. (*Maley & Taunton*)

A Glasgow tramcar at speed on the Coatbridge route on the private track segregated from the roadway though easily accessible to intending passengers. This line was opened in 1922. (*Glasgow Corporation Transport*)

Selly Oak to the Lickey Hills was opened the week before Whitsun 1924 and once again a transport undertaking was caught unawares with the new service being unable to cope with the mammoth queues; the general manager had not realised how much the populace needed a cheap ride out into lovely countryside. Every available tramcar was pressed into this new service; not all of them were in Birmingham's distinct blue livery, a few were open-topped cars, not seen in the city for years, and in a brown and cream livery which suggested that they had lain at the back of depots, long unused! Shorter sleeper-track extensions followed,

constructed on the median-strips as new roads became available.

Leeds was also a pioneer in segregated-tracks, with practically all the York Road lines on the east side of the city and sections of the routes to Lawnswood, Roundhay and Belle Isle using this system. The latter became linked with the direct line from the city to Middleton and was laid on private right-of-way, as was also the line to Temple Newsom, both being entirely separate from the roads. The Middleton Light Railway was unique in character and became a mecca for tramway and light railway students and enthusiasts. Leaving the highway in Moor Lane it ran alongside an historic colliery railway, on which Blenkinsop had experimented with his steam rack locomotive as early as 1812, and then ascended rapidly to pursue an extremely picturesque ride through Middleton

Two high capacity double-deck, totally enclosed Swansea & Mumbles bogie cars running on their private right-of-way track coupled together as multiple-units.

Woods. Middleton, with its huge housing estates was very elevated and exposed and on occasions when isolated by heavy snowfalls the Light Railway was its only connection with the city and served to carry provisions to this suburb. Leeds built a special fleet with the most modern equipment exclusively for this line, known locally as the 'Middleton bogies' because of their speed and comfort. They were double-deck bogie-cars and it was quite an experience to occupy the front seat in the upper saloon for the rapid glide down through Middleton Woods into the city.

Glasgow Corporation owned a number of tramways outside the city area, several of which were incorporated into the city system when the boundaries were enlarged, and some had sections of reserved-track. When the Airdrie & Coatbridge Tramways Company was taken over, the Corporation opened a splendid new roadside reserved-track section from Baillies to Coatbridge to connect the two systems. On the west of Glasgow, Paisley & District Tramways Company had a section of roadside reserved-track from Glenfield to Spiersbridge.

A curious example of early light railway construction was the Swansea and Mumbles Railway, the first railway in the world to carry passengers. Authorised by the Act of 29 June 1803 which read, 'The making and maintaining of a railway or Tramroad for the passage of wagons or other carriages to communicate with Swansea . . . and Oystermouth.' This Act also contained the odd wording that the '. . . hauling or drawing of the wagons or carriages was to be done by 'men, horses, *or otherwise*' and there can be little doubt that this was the earliest act to be framed in this manner. Horse-drawn passenger traffic started on 25 March 1807, preceding George Stephenson's Stockton & Darlington steam passenger train by nearly 20 years. After many vicissitudes, it was not until 1877 that steam-traction replaced the horses and having regard to the words '. . . or otherwise' in the original act no further authorisation by Parliament was necessary. It was not until March 1929 that this private right-of-way light railway was electrified and 13 double-deck bogie cars were purchased to work the line. They were the largest electric tramcars built for service in Britain with 106 seats and could be coupled in multiple with a maximum of 212 seats being available.

The Llandudno & Colwyn Bay Electric Railway owned a long coastal route mainly on private right-of-way, starting originally from Old Colwyn, then later from Colwyn Bay, through

Liverpool's 28 miles of segregated track out of its 97 route miles of tramway was the most extensive in Great Britain. (*R. J. S. Wiseman*)

Sunderland's excellent example of reserved track. (*Alan A. Jackson*)

Rhos-on-Sea and Penrhyn, thence over the Little Orme Head to Llandudno on a 3ft 6in gauge. In early days the company operated totally-enclosed single-deck cars of an 'inter-urban' American-type design but to cope with increased traffic in 1936 purchased ten double-deck cars from Bournemouth Corporation. When the line closed in 1956 it was the last company operated tramway in Britain.

Another little known example was the Portsdown & Horndean Light Railway which operated a fleet of double-deck open-top cars on a segregated footpath at the side of the London Road from Portsmouth to the village of Horndean. The track was partly elevated and had its own bridges spanning two side turnings, with through running from the South Parade Pier.

Better known to holiday makers is the 3ft gauge Isle of Man Electric Railway, which was constructed in 1893, is still operating and runs from Derby Castle, Douglas to Ramsey. This was a pioneer of the inter-urban American-type electric light railway using only single-deck bogie-cars entirely on reserved-track mostly away from the roadway, along a picturesque and scenic route, with the sea visible nearly all the way. In the summer trailer-cars are coupled to the tramcars and as this is the most direct route to Ramsey a small four-wheel luggage van is sometimes attached to the rear. Nearly 18 miles long, this line is unique in operating the same electric tramcars with which the line was opened in 1893, a tribute to the splendid servicing and maintenance by the workforce of dedicated tramwaymen in its works at Derby Castle.

Approximately half-way from Douglas to Ramsey is the unique Snaefell Mountain Electric Railway separately worked as the gauge in this

Speeding through the fields on its own right-of-way
is a single-deck Llandudno & Colwyn Bay bogie-car.

(*above*) Opening day of the Snaefell Mountain Tramway, Isle of Man, 21 August 1895 showing the cars in their unglazed condition at the temporary terminus outside Laxey depot. (*Mather & Platt*)

(*below*) The Manx Electric Light Railway follows the American type of inter-urban tramway both in its segregated track and rolling-stock. The illustration is of a bogie-car towing an open bogie-trailer at Derby Castle in 1894 on the 3ft gauge track. These same cars are still running in 1985. (*Mather & Platt*)

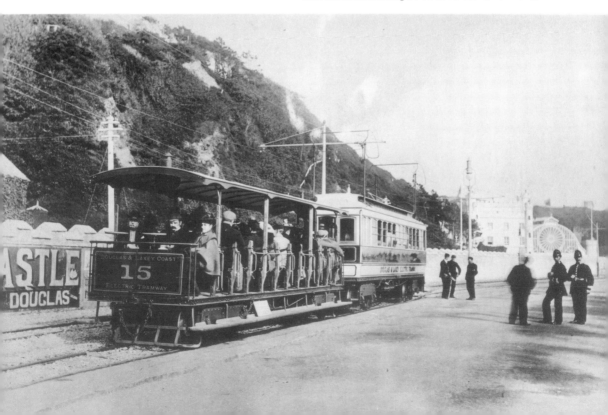

Snaefell Mountain Tramway motor-bogie complete
with 'gripper' brake for the 'Fell' rail in the centre.
(*Mather & Platt*)

case is 3ft 6in, with a fleet consisting of six totally-enclosed single-deck bogie-cars. On reserved-track it ascends gradients, in places of 1 in 12, to the top of Snaefell Mountain 2,034ft high, from which vantage point England, Scotland, Wales and Ireland can be seen on a clear day. A unique feature of this line of 4.62 miles is that it is equipped with a 'Fell' rail, named after its inventor. It consists of an ordinary running rail laid on its side between the running rails and slightly elevated, on which run extra horizontal wheels to obviate derailments. The cars are also equipped with additional braking shoes which grip this Fell rail on each side to assist the normal brakes of the car. Unlike the trolley-poles of the Manx Electric section, these six cars collect the current from the overhead wires by bow-collectors of an unusual design. The cars do not run to a fixed timetable and when the mountain is not shrouded in fog or mist, the stationmaster at the top phones down to Laxey for the service to commence operating. The cars ascend spirally in a clockwise direction round the mountain, reaching the hotel on top entirely by adhesion as distinct from rack-operation as would be normal with systems with these gradients. The service operates only in summer and the final mile or so of the trolley-wire is taken down from the traction-poles in winter to avoid damage from the exceptionally high winds.

One of the most curious electric tramway 'reservations' was owned by the Great Central Railway and ran from Immingham to Grimsby, which at the time were not easily accessible by road, and was constructed in 1912 when it was built at the same time as the docks. It was built with bull-head section rail except for the small street lengths where normal tramway rail was used and the rolling-stock consisted of extremely long bogie single-deck cars giving a half-hour service other than at shift times when convoys of additional cars were provided for the dock and factory workers.

During the later expansion of many existing termini numerous shorter lengths of the electric tramways were extended on private rights-of-way or segregated tracks, either on sleeper-track on the roadside or on the median-strips which divided dual carriageways. The great potential of this method of cheap light railway construction does not appear to have been fully appreciated at the time.

13

The Upsurge of the Rival Buses

The first motor buses, as a practical proposition for the conveyance of passengers, made a faltering start at the beginning of the century. One of the first operators was the Great Western Railway which started a service between Helston and the Lizard on 3 August 1903 with two low-powered motor vehicles; the Penzance to Newlyn service started soon afterwards. On 30 September 1904 Thomas Tilling commenced a service between Peckham and Oxford Circus; these Tilling buses had their bodies built by G. F. Milnes & Company Limited which had considerable experience in building tramcars, and the German firm of

Many petrol-driven motor-buses of this type were turned out in their early days. Limited to a speed of 12mph, their solid-rubber tyres and hard seats on the poor roads of that era was no help to passenger comfort.

Daimler built the chassis.

The London General Omnibus Company began its services in 1905 with only 20 motor buses working in London but expansion was so rapid that by 1908 its fleet had grown to 1,066; there were also various smaller private companies. In 1905 the British Electric Traction Company operated 15 double-deck buses in Birmingham which were subsequently taken over by the Birmingham & Midland Motor Omnibus Company, afterwards known as the 'Midland Red'. Other cities and towns saw the commencement of petrol-driven motor bus operation with the same small beginnings.

All these early buses had solid rubber tyres and with their springing and the state of the roads in their early days, left much to be desired, especially

as most of them were equipped with hard lath-type seats; certainly all the top decks were so equipped. In no way could a ride on these early buses be compared with the smooth rail-traction progression of the electric tramcar. They were also subject to frequent breakdowns and were slow and ungainly, and indeed, it was remarkable how some of the early double-deck buses, with their upper-decks of greater width than the rest of the bus, were ever permitted to operate because of their alarming swaying motion on uneven roads! Licensing control for passenger vehicles only existed in the major towns, which had the effect of protecting to some extent competition with the tramways. Buses were prevented from plying within municipal boundaries and although they could bring in passengers from outside, at return fares competitive with the tramways, they could not pick up and set down passengers within those boundaries.

The 1914—18 great war was a set-back for the buses as, although reliability was being improved, every gallon of petrol had to be imported into Britain despite German hostile action against the tankers on the high seas; this restricted bus operation accordingly. Moreover, buses were commandeered by the army for the use of troops; the London General Omnibus Company lost 1,600 buses alone and it took months to recover after hostilities had ceased. In May 1919 it had only 2,044 buses in daily service compared with 2,906 before the war in 1914. The tramcars coped with the additional traffic albeit with very heavy overcrowding. Glasgow, once described as the second city of the British Empire, with a normal tramways staff of 6,000 lost over 3,000 men sent overseas for service before 1918, and women not only conducted the tramcars but also drove some of them. The overcrowding can be viewed in perspective when it is realised that London County Council with 1,600 tramcars and 158 trailers, allowed in London from 1915 until 1924, had only 1,210 and 112 available for service during the war. All other British systems were similarly handicapped.

When the 1914—18 war ended thousands of unwanted army vehicles were sold at fantastically low prices, many from Hyde Park and others from an extensive dump at Slough. Some of the bus companies bought a quantity of these army-surplus vehicles, stripped off the bodies and used the chassis for their motor buses. Others, bought by demobilised men with their gratuities, received the same treatment, and were used to set themselves up as private bus operators.

Not only had the tramways suffered through lack of essential maintenance during the war, accentuated by being heavily overloaded, but many miles of track needed relaying, an expensive job which now had to be undertaken largely for the benefit of other road users.

At the beginning of the decade, 1918 to 1928, the competition from the buses had the effect of prompting the tramway undertakings to construct new and improved rolling stock and to make modifications to their existing fleets to obtain higher average speeds. This applied particularly in the cities where the magnetic track brakes were standard and gave quick and effective deceleration; the acceleration of an electric powered vehicle was vastly superior to those powered by petrol or diesel engines.

The year 1923 saw the advent of small pneumatic-tyred buses, generally operated by private operators. There was no Road Traffic Act and local authorities of urban district status and over could issue licences to drivers and conductors. Some operators simply bought a bus and started a service without local authority approval but matters were more closely controlled where the municipalities were operators of tramways or buses within their boundaries which they took good care to guard.

It was an entirely different story in many smaller towns where the local councils stupidly licenced any bus owner who chose to apply and thus created competition with its own existing electric tramways. A typical example is of one tramway, covering a wide area with 30 miles of track carrying 15,000,000 passengers a year with just over 100 tramcars, found itself suddenly in competition with a proliferation of privately-owned buses which paid no rates. The tramway paid no less than £10,000 a year in rates in addition to maintaining 30 miles of roadway at its own expense, and after serving densely populated areas with an efficient system was put out of business within a short period. The mentality of the councillors who so casually granted the bus licences, resulted in this double loss — rates of £10,000 a year and also the liability for maintaining the main roads — was astounding.

Another disastrous example of the phasing out of the electric tramway was the Corporation-owned system of the City of Kingston upon Hull, whose fleet comprised 180 tramcars in 1922 on 18 miles of track. It produced a revenue of £305,056 and carried $62\frac{1}{2}$ million passengers over 4 million miles, with senior citizens enjoying travel concessions. The first electric tram ran on 5 July 1899; the last horse tram ceased operating on 30 September of that year and the last steam tram on 13 January 1901. Outer sections of Hull's electric tramway ran on the reserved sleeper-track routes of Holderness Road, Beverley Road, Spring Bank West, Anlaby Road and Hessle Road. Under the co-ordination scheme of 1934 East Yorkshire Motor Services took over all these outer routes. Between 1938 and 1945 Hull tramways were replaced by trolleybuses except for Hedon Road which from 1932 had used motor buses. Trolleybuses were inaugurated on 23 July 1937 and the last electric tramcar completed 38 years of service to the city on 30 June 1945. The trolleybuses only lasted 24 years as they, in their turn, were phased out by petrol and then later diesel buses which were also operated jointly under the co-ordination scheme with the Corporation.

Although a number of electric tramway systems were closed from 1927 onwards, it was not until the 1930s that the biggest decline came. The peak number of over 14,000 tramcars in Britain was reduced by half to approximately 7,000.

Probably one of the most remarkably rapid abandonments of an extensive system over a wide area, embracing the vast conurbation of well-populated towns, was in the Black Country, where the system was controlled by the Birmingham & Midland Tramways Joint Committee. From 1914 its works at Tividale, near Dudley, had commenced building replacement tramcars to renew the fleets of the four companies under its control; although not time-expired the cars showed unmistakable signs of weaknesses due to the chronic overloading which had been allowed. The rebuilding programme, together with the addition of entirely new cars, was accelerated between 1919 and 1920 when a modern single-deck car, of a revolutionary design, being totally enclosed and having no interior bulkheads, made its appearance. It was designed to work on all routes, including those with low railway bridges. A

From 1925 onwards the small pneumatic-tyred bus of the type illustrated made its appearance and numbers of motor-garage proprietors usually purchased one or two of them to operate on tramway routes in the lucrative rush-hour periods. This type of opposition, with the improved comfort of pneumatic tyres over the former solid-rubber tyres attracted many of the tramway passengers; company-tramway undertakings in districts with sparse daytime traffic were early victims, and abandonments of their systems increased from 1927 onwards.

total of 42 of this modern type of tramcar was built, but most only ran for 10 years or less because of abandonments! In 1924/5 a number of privately-owned buses started operating on the tramway routes in direct competition. Some of these buses were quite small, 18 or 20 seaters, built on chassis supplied by the now defunct Bean Car Company of Dudley; others were of a larger type. The competing buses usually made their appearances only at times of heavy traffic, when workers were going to or coming from work, thus 'skimming the cream' of the business. Meanwhile the tramcars maintained their normal timetable service throughout the day, relying on the extra surge of passengers to and from work to balance the light traffic periods.

As the Birmingham & Midland Motor Omnibus Company Limited was a subsidiary of the Birmingham & Midland Tramways Joint Committee (B&MTJC) its aid was sought to mitigate the effect of the 'pirate' bus competition. They operated buses on routes not served by the tramways and where their routes overlapped had charged dearer fares avoiding competition with the tramways.

From 1 July 1924, the Birmingham & Midland Motor Omnibus Company (Midland Red) came on to the tram routes operated by the four companies comprising the B&MTJC. It introduced fleets of new pneumatic-tyred buses by agreement with the Tramway Committee and also with the various local authorities which owned other tramway tracks within their areas.

On some of the busier routes from which the 'pirate' buses were skimming the cream of the tramways, Midland Red, in addition to a normal service, also provided extra buses to 'nurse' the pirates; a Midland Red bus would follow a pirate bus closely and just before the next fare stage would overtake it and being at the stop first would take on board the queuing passengers. This type of 'grass-hopper' driving occasionally attracted the attention of the police and resulted in prosecutions for speeding and, in some cases, for dangerous driving.

Once Midland Red buses were on the tramway routes they could not be withdrawn and the Joint Committee decided that the tramways should be replaced by them, particularly as the competition was causing the services to be uneconomic. Agreements with the local authorities were negotiated and several of the pirate buses were bought out by Midland Red and others withdrew under intensified competition.

Although the example given concerns the extensive tramway system in the Midlands, it is typical of what happened elsewhere in scores of situations where the electric tramways became threatened by pirate buses. One strange aspect was that, in very many cases, the actual scheduled timetables of the tramcars were the same as the competing buses!

14

The Second World War Scene

Those cities and towns which had not discarded their tramways before the second world war benefitted by their foresight to a considerable degree. They were fortunate in being able to rely on a passenger transport system dependent on home-produced fuel, coal, whereas the bus services relied on fuel which had to come by sea where hostile action resulted in many oil-tankers being sunk. Consequently with the shortage of fuel bus services became restricted and many of them ceased running in the evenings, whereas the electric tramways were able to maintain their services throughout the war and provided a reasonable evening service.

In the unlit blacked-out cities there was something reassuring about the tramway. The shining tramway lines were there, the overhead wires were there and to a serviceman on leave, arriving by a late train it was very welcome when the sound of an approaching tramcar could be heard and its darkened bulk loomed out of the night to complete his journey home. No such assurance was evident on bus routes which with the absence of any permanent-way, the vehicle crawled along the dark streets with only its tiny faint headlights to guide the driver – if, indeed, it

In common with the rest of the country, tramways suffered casualties. Bedminster depot, Bristol after the blitz of 3–4 January 1941. (*Bristol Omnibus Company*)

turned up at all.

The black-out was far more severe than in the first world war as in 1914–18 headlights and interior lights were only shaded downwards, to prevent observation by Zeppelins and in the South East occasional enemy planes. Only a few of either penetrated the defences compared with the 1939–45 war when air raids were very heavy over much of the country. All vehicles were restricted to considerably dimmed headlights but, being rail-borne, tramcars benefitted and were able to attain higher speeds with safety. Interior lights on tramcars and buses were no more than a dim glow. To prevent an occasional flash being visible from above, tramway overhead trolley-wires had to be equipped with 'arc-shields' in certain places, mainly on the section-insulators which occurred at half-mile distances to feed the current into the trolley-wires from the main feed-cables underground. Most track and overhead maintenance could only be done by daylight and with a staff shortage maintenance of both tracks and vehicles was neglected. By 1945 the tramcars, which had been worked to the limit, were in a rather sorry condition.

Street lamps were unlit and although there was a general 20mph speed limit the tramcars had the advantage as a seasoned driver could tell by the noise of the wheels on the rails exactly where he was. On curves the wheels made a humming noise and the trolley-wheels also made a different noise on the overhead trolley wires and at a section-insulator the lights would briefly go out and then on again, all indicating to the driver various locations on the route. Other road vehicles had no such assistance; the tramcar would always get one home, in fog or blackout!

When the air-raid warning sirens sounded, drivers were under instructions to stop and direct the passengers to the nearest air-raid shelter; a list was provided for each route. Usually the passengers enquired, 'Are you going on, driver?' and getting an affirmative reply, they invariably would say 'In that case we're stopping on!' The tramcar would proceed on its way, picking up and setting down passengers to the accompaniment of distant, and sometimes not so distant, bangs and flashes on the ground and in the sky with the pencilled beams from the searchlights criss-crossing the blackness!

In addition to damage to rolling stock by bomb blast with tramcars often in service with boarded-up windows as glass was practically unobtainable and lacked regular painting, the tracks and

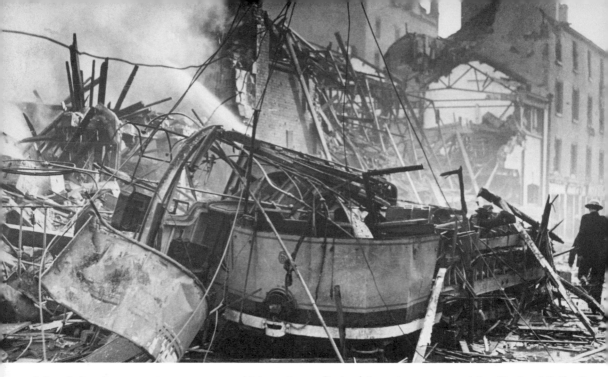

(*above*) Another casualty, a tramcar which took a direct hit from a bomb in Nelson Street, Glasgow, with heavy casualties during the Clydeside blitz on 14 March 1941. Incredibly this tramcar was subsequently rebuilt at Glasgow Corporation's renowned Coptlawhill works and put back into service. (*Glasgow Corporation Transport*)

(*below*) A post-war scene at the Elephant & Castle, London, the wrecked buildings illustrating the extent of the war-time damage with which tramcars had to contend to maintain the service. This picture shows three 'Felthams' and two London standard cars. It indicates at this busy junction how well tracks survived such a long period of restricted maintenance with only occasional 'first aid' and blitz repairs. (*London Transport*)

overhead wires also suffered. 'Short-working' had to be resorted to when a bomb damaged the tracks and cars had to operate to and from each side of a crater with the passengers walking to change cars. It was remarkable how quickly repairs were made, sometimes in half the time it would normally have taken, tracks were relaid and the service restored after a bombing. To 'keep the service going' the crater would be filled in and reasonably compacted down and a single line laid, a 'pilotman' or an inspector controlling the passage of the cars over the single-track until the other one had been repaired.

An interesting instruction issued to the tramcar-crews in London during the blitz stated: 'Damage to Tracks. Enemy Action. In order that services may be restored as soon as possible after enemy action it may be necessary in some cases for tramcars to run over skeleton (unpaved) track. During the black-out a red lamp will be placed at each end of such open track and, before a car can proceed, the Conductor must remove the red lamps and, after the passage of the car, replace the lamps in position on the track'. No easy task stumbling over rubble in the blackout!

When one line was damaged by bombing, it was sometimes possible for a car to reverse over a trailing crossover and proceed on the undamaged line – 'wrong road working' – before rejoining the correct line beyond the damage. When this happened a pilotman travelled on the car over the single-line in one direction then changed to another car travelling in the opposite direction. This obviated the possibility of two cars meeting on a single-track as no car could proceed without the pilotman. In some areas it was possible to use diversions over alternative routes to circumvent the bomb damage until it was repaired.

At the end of the war several tramway systems had fewer cars in service than at the beginning and this was quite difficult to explain, for although some cars were lost through bomb damage there were many serviceable cars in the depots. London Transport, for example, had only a maximum of 734 cars in service when the war finished, 10% fewer than in 1941. It appears that no real attempt was made to increased tramcar mileage directly to replace lost bus mileage, nor to increase the tramcars in service to make up for the reduced speeds due to the blackout and the fact that 23% more passengers were carried between 1943 and 1945 than in 1941.

Some tramways were closed by war damage,

Some cities employed women drivers. Considering the weight of a tramcar (anything up to 20 tons) this demonstrates the ease with which such a heavy vehicle can be controlled by air, regenerative and magnetic track brakes. In February 1941 Glasgow trained the first group of 26 motorwomen, and this number was increased as the war dragged on. Above is a Glasgow motorwoman in 1942 and, judging by her happy smile, seen in the passenger mirror above her, she is obviously well in control and enjoying tramcar driving. (*Glasgow Corporation Transport*)

for example Bristol which, as we have seen, never ran again. An emergency bus service was substituted the following day. After Coventry's terrible air-raid of 1940, the whole tramway system was abandoned quite unexpectedly because although the rolling-stock and depots were spared much damage and the tracks repaired, the main damage was to the feeder cables, and replacement buses, borrowed from most of the neighbouring towns were quickly brought into service.

The outbreak of war in 1939 gave a new lease of life to Manchester's tramways and overhead trolley-wires were quickly erected on previously closed routes and the services restored. Manchester's trams suffered little damage from air-raids although large sections of the city were devastated.

Birmingham, an industrial city, was possibly not intended to be indiscriminately bombed, but with the lack of accuracy certainly was. Apart from actual damage, many routes were temporarily suspended due to debris, fire hoses across the tracks or the presence of unexploded bombs, in some cases. An ingenious ramp was devised which could be placed on the tram lines for the cars to ride over the fire hoses. On 4 December 1940 Witton depot received a direct hit, destroying many tramcars, and on the night of 9/10 April 1941 separate bombs again damaged the city's tramways, the most serious being a direct hit on Miller Street depot where 27 cars were completely

destroyed with another four at Washwood Heath depot. A programme of dispersal was then put into effect, cars being parked overnight at various termini, on reserved-tracks or at other points to minimise loss in the event of depots being bombed.

The second world war brought with it the destruction of much of Southampton by enemy air raids as thousands of army vehicles were using this port. Strange things happen in war and, considering the tremendous damage to Southampton, only one tramcar and one bus were lost due to enemy action, the tramcar by an incendiary bomb! As elsewhere, tramcars were in service with bullet or shrapnel holes, windows repaired with canvas or three-ply wood as well as the tracks and overhead wires being frequently damaged. A programme of nightime dispersal was also introduced here.

The air raids on Glasgow were for some time surprisingly light compared with those of London and other cities, but in the spring of 1941, from 15–28 March, Clydeside became the centre of several heavy 'blitzes' and it was not until 7 April that tramcars which had been stranded in Clydebank for some weeks because of craters, were recovered.

Throughout the war years many women conductresses, or 'clippies' as they were called, were employed by the tramways in Britain. As well as the men they showed tremendous courage and endurance under the appalling conditions created by the blitz, the V1 flying bombs and V2 rockets.

15

Unfair Competition and Decline

After the cessation of hostilities in 1945 the time came to take stock of the state of the electric tramways which had given unrivalled service in British cities throughout the war – and which, moreover, had their source of power from home-produced fuel. Against almost overwhelming odds they had to operate on a 'make do and mend' policy and it was obvious that the sadly neglected maintenance of the past six years had to be made good. They still had to contend with the clause in the Tramways Act of 1870 which stated that they

had to pave and maintain the road surface between their tracks and for 18in on each side. In the case of double-track routes this meant that tramway undertakings had to maintain huge areas of roadway which they did not use, for the benefit of other road users, including their competitors, the buses. This grievous and injurious Act had already had a disastrous effect in whittling-down practically all the company-owned tramways and an overwhelming number of the corporation systems before the war and was now, after the war, seen to

One of the most remarkable post-war abandonment policies was that of Aberdeen. Four excellent modern double-deck tramcars were constructed in 1940 followed by another 20 after the war up to 1949. Two were four-wheel cars and the remaining 22 were bogie cars with centre-entrances. All were double-deck cars of high capacity designed to run on the wide trunk road of the Bridge of Dee to the Bridge of Don route. Despite these recent additions of streamlined cars to an existing reliable fleet, the extravagent decision to abandon the tramways of Aberdeen was taken and the last tramcar ran on 3 May 1958. The whole of the fleet was scrapped, including the foregoing splendid tramcars, 20 of which were not ten years old. (*R. B. Parr*)

be a big obstacle to the reinstatement and relaying of damaged and worn track. The fact that the electric tramways throughout the war had rendered sterling service to our main cities which had retained them was soon forgotten.

There were 35 electric tramway systems running at the end of the war, varying from a few cars to upwards of 1,000 or more. After London had completed its conversion in 1952 only 13 of these were left and another three went by 1955, including Sunderland – which 25 years previously had been regarded as a stalwart tramway town – and Liverpool – which in the 1930s had introduced a successful policy of modernisation – both decided to change to buses. Glasgow dithered, mainly because of local politics, until 1962 because its unified service was regarded with affection by the populace. It had undertaken tramway route extensions in 1949 and with 100 of the finest cars of advanced design, built at the Coptlawhill works, had a system to be proud of. The city had also rebuilt its power station between 1948–9 at an enormous cost and this had escaped nationalisation. Glaswegians felt so strongly about their trams that at a meeting of the full council the casting vote of the Lord Provost was required to

carry the motion to convert only one route to buses.

One of the saddest closures of a tramway system in the post-war period was that of Aberdeen. Four excellent totally-enclosed modern double-deck cars were constructed in 1940 followed by another 20 after the war between 1945 and 1949. Two were four-wheel cars and the remaining 22 were bogie cars with centre entrances and high passenger capacity, designed to run on the wide trunk road of the Bridge of Dee to Bridge of Don route. Despite the recent additions of these streamlined cars to an existing fine and reliable fleet, the amazing and extravagant decision to abandon the tramways in Aberdeen was taken and the last tramcar ran on 3 May 1958. The whole of the fleet was scrapped, including those 24 splendid tramcars, some not even ten years old! It was a despicable example of myopic local politics and a wanton waste of ratepayers' money.

Rising costs caught the tramways at a big disadvantage. In 1950 the cost of new rails was some 60 per cent higher than pre-war and the cost of electricity about 50 per cent higher. A big factor in influencing local councils was that in 1950 a new

Tramcars were welcomed by motorists in foggy weather, as keeping to a predetermined track they were followed by a procession of cars, lorries and even the few motor-buses which had not been withdrawn from service in the fog, in addition to guaranteeing to get their own passengers home. (*Glasgow Corporation Transport*)

tramcar might cost anything up to £10,000 while a new bus could be purchased for about £4,000. Councillors did not stop to reflect that while the life of a bus was, at that time, about 12 to 14 years, the life of a tramcar, as proved by many in service, was quite 40 years – at the time of abandonment of tramways in Glasgow 85 per cent of Glasgow's fleet was 35 years or more of age with 50 of their cars being 40–45 years old, 320 being 45–50 years old and 200 were more than 50 years old! All its fleet had, of course, been modernised over the years and by re-equipping them with modern motors had speeded up the service to a marked degree.

British electric tramway systems were subjected to intense pressure to accelerate their demise by the petrol, diesel and rubber-tyre barons. The conduct of some of the local councillors in our great cities who assisted in the disposal of municipally-owned tramways, a valuable national asset of such magnitude, was the cause of considerable public disquiet. It should also be recorded that whereas fares on the tramways often remained unrealistically low there was a 'revision' upwards when buses took over – a 'revision' which has continued ever since accompanied by ever-reducing bus services.

Tramcars carried record numbers of passengers during the war and for several years afterwards because of the small number of private cars and the petrol for them. About 1949–50 traffic began to fall in the recession and the number of privately-owned buses declined; misled by the post-war boom many operators had committed themselves heavily to hire-purchase, found it difficult to maintain payments, and many ceased operating. The bus companies then entered a vicious circle which still continues; the more that services are reduced and fares raised, the fewer passengers they carry; even with government and local authority subsidies they experience difficulty in balancing their books – a vicious circle. Of course the growth in private car use has played a large part.

16

Fighting for its Life — the Incursion of the Private Car

During the period of 1948–60 financial results weighed heavily against the British tramcar. Previously showing a handsome profit and in the case of corporation tramways relieving the rates in no small measure, the cost of operating, maintenance and purchase of new rolling stock soon overtook receipts. Liverpool and Glasgow reported heavy losses in the 1950–51 period. For British tramways as a whole average receipts in this period remained at 23.5 (old) pence (10p) per car mile but expenditure increased to between 24 and 25.7 pence per mile, thus supporting a strong case for replacing them.

Another aspect also came to the fore. Tramcars had drawn their electricity from municipally-owned power stations and with the advent of the nationalised electricity industry in 1948, locally-owned power stations became superfluous as electricity could be produced in bulk far cheaper than by these smaller power stations. However the generating boards charged users normal commercial prices, which were often higher than the local power stations.

At this time the problem of congestion was well to the fore. Road traffic was sparse before and during the war but as motor cars proliferated, the tramcar, because it occupied fixed tracks along the centre of the street, held up other traffic while loading and unloading its passengers. Much was made of this safety angle from the passengers' viewpoint.

Town-planning authorities replanning towns after the devastation of the war regarded tramcars with abhorrence. Reserved tracks to segregate the

An example of moving crowds. Two London tramcars loading on the always well patronised Victoria Embankment, with London soldiering on with its pre-war cars, pursuing a policy of 'make do and mend' until the final bus takeover in 1952. It was a tribute to the robustly-built tramcars and soundly-constructed tracks and electrical equipment which, after five and a half years of scantily maintained war service, were called on for another seven years' wear until the buses were built. (*London Transport*)

London's Kingsway Subway which connected the tramway systems north and south of the river followed the line of two new streets built in the early part of the century. Although sanctioned in 1902 it was not opened until 1905/8 for single-deck cars and deepened to take double-deck cars in 1930/31.

It provided a fast and frequent service between the Embankment and Bloomsbury, the running time between the latter point and Westminster Underground station being seven minutes, a really fast run by any standards. The illustration is of Holborn tramway station. (*London Transport*)

tramcars were not as feasible in city centres as they were in the suburbs, as the cost would be prohibitive, so the tramcars had to continue using the centre of the streets exactly as they had been doing since the dawn of the century. Tramcars were inflexible and could not load at the kerbside as could buses but an outstanding attempt was made to overcome this disadvantage in Birmingham. Despite the strong opposition of the Tramways General Manager, the Chief Constable persuaded the City Council to realign the rails at busy loading-points to the kerbside. Whilst overcoming to some extent passengers holding up other traffic this innovation was in itself, a traffic hazard. It was in the days before trafficators were installed on road vehicles to indicate an intended change of direction and although local Birmingham car drivers would possibly know when a tramcar was suddenly going to lurch to the left without warning, other drivers not familiar with the roads would not. As the General Manager anticipated and the Chief Constable did not, there were quite a number of accidents due to this purely local peculiarity.

Another disadvantage was that when the tramways were built there were situations where the roadway was not wide enough to allow the rails to be laid in the centre of the highway because other road traffic, mainly horse-drawn, could not pass the cars. In such cases the rails were laid to one side of the highway where, particularly on single-line sections the tramcar in one direction was compelled to proceed against the normal traffic flow. Not only was this dangerous on straight roads, especially in foggy weather, but more so at corners where a motor car driver on his correct side of the road would suddenly be confronted with a tram looming up at him in the opposite direction, a highly alarming situation.

In the narrowest streets a procession of cars and lorries would often accumulate behind the tram when it stopped to load as they were unable to overtake it due to the width of the roadway, before its next stop. In a few cases where the highway narrowed and the tramcar veered towards the pavement an unwary motorist had to brake suddenly to avoid being trapped between the tram and the kerb so signs, 'Tram Pinch', were installed by the Ministry of Transport to give warning of this hazard.

Local authorities were not disposed to do anything to improve the situation even where improvement was possible. Sometimes where improvements were made in the highway, the tramcar was not allowed to share in them as in the case where one-way systems were inaugurated;

the track layout was not altered and, again, the tramcar was left to take a contra-flow route against normal traffic. In contrast was the new roundabout system alongside County Hall in London complete with new tram tracks, all for nothing since the trams were withdrawn just a few weeks later.

Few of the remaining operators purchased any new tramcars; the wartime slogan of 'make do and mend' still applied to those in service after the war, even though some of them had travelled well over 1,000,000 miles and were 40 to 50 years old. An example is a fleet of Birmingham tramcars delivered to the corporation in 1913 and when scrapped in 1952 each had attained over this mileage, in fact two had exceeded 1,200,000 miles and six, more than 1,150,000 miles. During their 39 years of service they had undergone various modifications and improvements to keep them going, such as higher horse-power motors, enclosed upper-deck canopies and upholstered reversable seats in the lower saloon. Birmingham also operated 'newer' cars and although in service for only 26 years some had travelled 856,600 miles before going for scrap.

This record of long-life and comparatively trouble-free service was apparent in those cities which had retained their trams although in London the tram fleet, in 1946, under the ownership of the London Passenger Transport Board, was suffering from wartime neglect. In that year on 15 November it was announced that the remaining tramways would be replaced, not by trolleybuses as was the original intention, but by diesel buses. A Government Minister said at the time, '. . . this had to be done, otherwise to refurbish London's tramways would tie us to tramcars for the next twenty years'. Conversion was to commence within five years and it was estimated that 1,100 new buses would be needed to replace 800 tramcars; the die was cast.

There were still so many restrictions and so many shortages of consumer goods that before the new buses could be constructed to replace the tramcars, it would take five years to renew the existing bus fleet which was also in a very run-down state. In 1946 913 tramcars were still operating in London on 102 route miles, with 1,747 trolleybuses in service on 255 route miles. Now that it was known that the tramcars were reprieved for another five years, more cars were renovated and it was a sorry sight to see them in service fitted with strengthening tie bars in the lower saloons to offset structural weaknesses caused by overloading during wartime years. Improvements to the track also continued to be made until the final demise of London's electric tramcars on 5 July 1952. Other cities closed their tramway systems a few years later: Sunderland in 1954, Dundee and Edinburgh in 1956, Aberdeen in 1958, Leeds in 1959, Sheffield in 1960 and Glasgow, the last of the big urban systems in 1962. Blackpool, the first and now the last on the mainland, and the Isle of Man were the only ones left operating electric tramway systems in Great Britain.

In the years immediately preceding the first world war, when the electric tramcar was 'King of the Road', there were only 200,000 motor vehicles in Britain compared to the year preceding the second world war when motor-vehicles had risen to over 3,000,000. Today in contrast, it is stated to be 16 million or more and has resulted in a further decline in public transport; the ubiquitous motor car has succeeded in defeating its own primary purpose that of transporting its owner quickly and cheaply from his home into the city. The discomfort and wasted hours caused by sitting immobilised in cars delayed by mammoth traffic-jams on inadequate roads, burning up expensive fuel by engines ticking-over is a frustration compared with which the delays formerly caused by electric tramcars pale into insignificance. Moreover, with the passage of time, it is obvious that the wheel has turned its full cycle as the former 'inflexibility of tramcars' with their fixed tracks has now been substituted by marked-off defined 'bus lanes' to enable the present-day public transport system to make any reasonable progress at all!

17

What Might Have Been

Having decided that electric tramcars were obsolete and an impediment to other road traffic in Britain and in consequence having abandoned our electric tramways, torn up all the tracks and consigned all the rolling-stock to funeral-pyres in tramway graveyards, it is pertinent to examine why neighbouring countries took a different view and did not do likewise. While Britain employed all its efforts in disposing of this valuable national asset, without any serious attempt to adapt or modernise them to the changing patterns of the towns, continental cities and towns examined their own passenger transport problems in commendably greater depth. It was noticeable that most countries which had suffered occupation during the war, unlike Britain, were loath to rely so heavily on the politically unstable Middle-East for their fuel and did not want to put all their eggs in one basket for having their passenger transport

An eight-axle articulated modern three-unit electric tramcar for the Mannheim—Heidelberg system, Germany, built by Düwag of Düsseldorf. This firm can build a complete tramcar every 1½ days; a tramcar in Germany can be a 2, 4, 6, 8 or 12-axle vehicle. (*Düwag, Düsseldorf*)

wholly dependent on oil.

The largest electric tramway systems now operating in the world are in the cities of Leningrad, Vienna and Budapest. Systems are also operating in Holland, Belgium, Austria, Portugal, Norway, Sweden, Finland, East and West Germany, Poland, Switzerland, Italy and Hungary. What is becoming the largest and most efficient expanding system is the unification of the various undertakings in Ruhr conurbation to form a vast network of electric tramways.

The intense aerial bombing of the industrial area of the Ruhr, caused the various German tramway undertakings to lose much of their track, rolling stock and buildings. In 1943 bomb damage was so heavy that transport of war workers by tramcar to and from the factories broke down completely and it was decided to develop a new wartime utility tramcar the *Kriegs Strassenbahnwagen* or KSW as it became universally known. These were four-wheel cars with steel bodies and a minimum of seats, with only three side-windows but exceptionally long platforms, the intention being to carry large numbers of standing passengers.

At the end of the war in 1945, German electric tramways were in a hopeless position with their layouts completely disabled and their rolling stock seriously damaged and depleted. Cologne, Essen and Oberhausen for example, lost 40 per cent of their rolling stock and the rubble-strewn streets and heavily damaged tracks prevented tramway operation on numerous routes until urgent repairs had been carried out.

Contrast this situation with our own at the cessation of hostilities. Bristol and Coventry had entirely lost their tramways through bombing but the remaining systems which we had retained, were in working order mostly with adequate rolling stock. Completely failing to appreciate the value of the sterling service our own electric tramways had given the war effort, we set about examining how quickly we could dispense with this reliable and competent form of public transport!

One traveller by road in May 1946, a year after

hostilities ceased, records that from The Hague to Prague, using a different route on his return during a total of 1,445 miles, he saw only 13 motor buses east of Nijmegen even though some town tramways, notably Würzburg and Bonn, were still out of action. The systems in Frankfurt and west of the river in Cologne were working, although there were heaps of rubble alongside many of the tracks. On the whole the German tramways made a remarkably quick recovery, greatly helped by the standardization of design for new cars. The German utility KSW tramcar lasted well into the 1970s when it was replaced by more modern cars; it was used in the later years mainly for rush hour traffic.

In Germany where by law tramcars have priority over other road users, tramways were regarded as one of their greatest urban passenger transport assets and it became government policy to encourage electricity in preference to imported fuel. Advantage was also taken of the widespread devastation to widen the roads on rebuilding in order to provide greater facilities for future road traffic, whereas in Britain many ruined buildings were rebuilt to their former building-lines thus accentuating existing traffic difficulties and making the retention and up-grading of the remaining electric tramways more difficult.

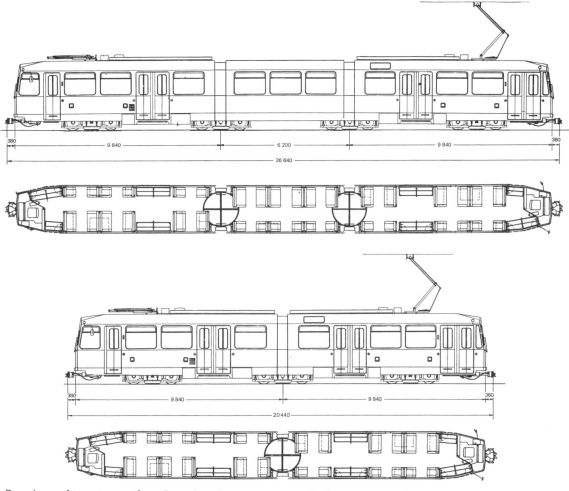

Drawings of two types of modern electric tramcars built by Düwag of Düsseldorf for many present-day German tramway systems. The eight-axle articulated tramcar (top) accommodates 310 passengers seated and standing during rush hours and offers a number of seats in light-traffic hours. The six-axle articulated car's capacity is 250 passengers at times of heavy traffic, with 36 seats at other times. Both cars are one-man operated with pre-booking of fares from kiosks or ticket machines.

In contrast again, war-devastated Germany seized the opportunity presented by their extended new house building programme in their suburbs to construct expanding electric tramway systems on segregated tracks on the median-strip dividing the new highways, on which to operate rapid-transit high-speed streamlined tramcars of advanced design.

In Britain we have concentrated on building motorways, very commendable when the priority is getting from A to B quickly but not so commendable when the car-owner is confronted by heavy city traffic congestion thus neutralising all the time saved. In Zurich the Swiss were faced with an identical problem. Instead of spending vast sums of money on widening streets and installing large car-parks in the centre of the city to accommodate even more motor-cars, they have spent their money more wisely by modernising and up-grading their electric tramways to attain higher speeds, installing car-parks at all tramway termini and segregating tramcar tracks where possible. As a result one parks one's car in these parks on the periphery of Zurich and takes a cheap and rapid tramcar to the centre of the city, thus obviating both traffic frustration and the inevitable search for highly priced car parks.

Utrecht abandoned its electric tramways in 1938, but over the past few years has reinstated them constructing two main inter-urban routes, mainly on segregated track, from the town centre to outlying suburbs where housing has expanded. Here the Dutch have taken advantage of the lessons they learned in Amsterdam and Rotterdam where the new tramways were expanded with modern rapid-transit tramcars.

In the 1950s the argument against the tramcars in Britain was simple. With the exception of Glasgow, Aberdeen, Liverpool and Leeds much of the rolling-stock was 25 years old or more and would be costly to replace. The track, long neglected, also required considerable expenditure. Oil was cheap and buses were seen as faster and more flexible. No-one then talked of 'bus lanes' or foresaw that buses would be impeded as acutely by the private car as was the tramway system.

That Britain is an island need not be just a geographical fact but can also be an attitude of mind. Even as we scrapped our electric tramways because they were old and worn out, also when they weren't — as notably in Aberdeen — cities in exactly the same situation as ours, not only in the Netherlands, Belgium, Austria, Switzerland and especially in Germany but virtually in the whole of Eastern Europe took a different view and modernised.

There is no doubt that a fair hearing for Light Rapid Transit (the modern name for electric tramways) was impossible in the 1950s. Britons still believed that what they did was right and were not interested in what was happening in Hanover or Amsterdam or Düsseldorf.

18

The National Tramway Museum

When electric tramcars were fast disappearing from our streets in the 1950s a band of dedicated enthusiasts got together with the idea of preserving a number of them for posterity and eventually to construct a tramway museum. They formed the 'Tramway Museum Society', supported by funds from like-minded enthusiasts, to keep alive the form of street passenger transport which had served this country so well.

It was not until 1959, after a long and exhausting search for a suitable site, that the Society acquired what was then part of a derelict limestone quarry at Crich, near Matlock in Derbyshire. This quarry was originally developed by George Stephenson the railway pioneer, who built a narrow-gauge mineral railway to link the quarry with the main line at Ambergate.

The early financial difficulties of these preservation pioneers were considerable as tramcars from abandoned lines were purchased immediately they became available, transported to Crich by road and then sheeted down under tarpaulins to await the purchase and erection of suitable depots. More funds had then to be collected as quickly as possible, for electric tramcars left in the open at the mercy of the elements on an exposed site in Derbyshire, under tarpaulins, soon deterioriated. The need for depots was urgent.

By dint of very hard work from volunteers, in

fund raising and acquiring the necessary buildings, then levelling and preparing the foundations on the site, the depots were eventually erected and the tramcars, many serviceable and in good condition, were put under permanent cover. Then came the task of tracklaying, erecting the overhead trolley-wires, installing an electric power supply, building a workshop and securing spare parts, because from the beginning the Society was determined to have a working Museum and demonstrate its cars in action.

Along part of the track-bed of George Stephenson's former railway, volunteer members of the Society, drawn from all walks of life, now spend their spare time and holidays helping to consolidate and operate this replica electric tramway. In addition to about 50 tramcars, all built between 1873 (horse-drawn) and 1953, there is a mile long tramway built by them, fully operational and available for visitors to the Museum to experience the joys of riding on one of this country's erstwhile electric tramcars with the bonus of beautiful scenic views across the Derwent valley.

At the entrance to the Museum a townscape typical of the early tramway period, has been constructed, since it was thought appropriate to display the tramcars in their original settings. Stone paving, setts, Victorian gas lamps and other street furniture together with an Edwardian bandstand have been installed so accurately that they are frequently used by film and television

(*top*) An early LCC open-top tramcar arriving at the Town End terminus at the National Tramway Museum at Crich, near Matlock, Derbyshire, showing the townscape, typical of the Edwardian period with stone paving and Victorian gas-lamps. This LCC car No 106 was restored by an enthusiastic band of London members and transported to Crich in 1983. The memorial to the Sherwood Foresters can be seen in the background (*G. B. Claydon*)

(*middle*) Former Blackpool Corporation tramcar No 40 seen loading at Town End, Crich. The destination-box indicates one of its former routes. (*G. B. Claydon*)

(*bottom*) A former Glasgow Corporation car, restored at Crich, seen arriving from Wakebridge. The rear of the imposing Assembly Rooms, donated by Derby Corporation and re-sited at Crich can be seen on the right of the picture. (*G. B. Claydon*)

89

companies requiring 'period' scenes in their production.

The National Tramway Museum is an educational charity and each year is visited by thousands, including children's guided tours conducted by its members round the depots and exhibitions. When one considers that some countries like Switzerland, France and Austria have provided tramway museums out of public funds, Crich is a great credit to those enthusiasts who, by their perseverance and determination and with comparatively little help from public sources, have saved so many of our electric tramcars in this splendid museum for the enlightenment and entertainment of present and future generations.

The façade of the imposing Assembly Rooms was donated by Derby Corporation and re-sited at the museum, stone by stone, where it serves as a tramways' exhibition area on the ground floor with a library and an archive on the upper floors. On the front of the façade a plaque which was unveiled by HRH The Duke of Gloucester, Patron of the Tramway Museum Society, in 1976, marks the rebuilding.

Near the depot complex is a portion of track equipped with the stud contact system. There are also examples of different types of traction poles, overhead trolley-wires, types of suspension together with complex trackwork, points and crossings, many in use, some simply on display.

In addition to this extensive museum at Crich, there are smaller systems which have managed to preserve one or two tramcars; at Beamish, County Durham; Carlton Colville, Lowestoft; Heaton Park, Manchester; and at the Black Country Museum at Dudley, West Midlands. At Seaton, Devon, half-size replica tramcars on a 2ft 9in gauge provide a tourist service between the town and the neighbouring villages of Colyford and Colyton. Neither at the National Tramway Museum nor at the other tourist-attraction tramways must the visitor expect the preserved tramcars to reach the speeds attained when they were in regular use as the overriding consideration is to preserve them with care for posterity, especially when one considers the difficulties encountered when acquiring them and the hard work entailed in their restoration. Some cities and towns also have managed to restore and exhibit one of their former electric tramcars as a static exhibit in their local museum. Former Metropolitan Electric Tramways 'Feltham' type car No. 355 has been restored to its original pristine condition and is now exhibited in the London Regional Transport Museum at Covent Garden together with other cars. Birmingham car No 395 is preserved in the Museum of Science and Technology while Glasgow has preserved tramcars in its Transport Museum. A number of tramcars from their former electric tramway systems are also preserved in museums in various towns where they once provided an efficient passenger transport service for many years.

19

Renascence and Future Prospects

In Great Britain a technology gap in urban transport exists between the bus and urban railway. Other countries have bridged that gap very successfully with 'Light Rail Transit' (LRT), an internationally accepted term but more easily understood in Britain as a 'modern tramway'. As buses reach the limit of their development, at least so far as capacity and staffing levels are concerned and the conventional heavyweight urban railway becomes too expensive to build in all but the largest and wealthiest cities of the world, the scope for completely new light rail transit installations as an alternative to the better known modes of transit, which may be inadequate or over expensive, has

come to the fore.

The diesel bus seemingly has the lowest operating costs of any public transport system since it is operated on the public highway and, apart from taxes, is charged nothing for that privilege, a privilege limited because it must share the highway with other road users, competing for space on equal terms. As a result average speeds in urban areas are low, resulting in poor productivity in terms of vehicles and staff and unattractive services for the passenger, consequently the perennial problem of falling patronage and increased congestion due to private car traffic is exacerbated.

A six-axle car drawing a trailer on the Krefeld–Düsseldorf route halted at a loading point on its segregated track. (*Olaf Guttler*)

The latest double-deck bus now being produced is a little different from those produced 25 years ago. Use on the highway limits its size to that of a box normally 10m long (32ft 10in), 2.5m (8ft 2in) wide and 4.4m (14ft 5in) high, accommodating some 80 seated passengers and operated by one person. With one-person operation approaching 100 per cent on many undertakings and staff comprising some 70 per cent of operating costs, further economy by handling the passengers in an efficient and comfortable manner with fewer staff is out of the question and therefore, any increased patronage can only be accommodated with a corresponding increase in the number of vehicles and staff. It is true that there is interest in the articulated bus as a solution but this relies for its high capacity on a high proportion of standing passengers, which could not be accommodated safely on a double-deck vehicle. Apart from some specialised applications large numbers of standing passengers on a bus are not advisable from the viewpoint of both comfort and safety.

The simple arithmetic of multiplying the maximum frequency by vehicle capacity will show that it is difficult to carry more than 6,000 passengers per hour per direction by a bus and even this requires ideal conditions which seldom exist.

The conventional railway in its urban application is normally found in two forms, firstly as a service provided by a national authority often over tracks shared with long-distance trains, although sometimes on its own tracks, and second as a heavy rapid transit system, and 'underground' or metro, totally segregated from other rail services and usually operated by a separate authority, often a municipal enterprise such as Glasgow Underground. The *heavy* metro is ideal for carrying very large traffic flows at high average speeds between widely spaced stops, staff productivity is high and increased automation is possible. But the higher average speed is at the expense of poorer access for the population due to the widely spaced stops. 15,000 passengers per hour per direction is generally regarded as the minimum traffic flow to justify new heavy metro construction.

Light Rail Transit is a mode which can deal economically with traffic flows of between 2,000 and 20,000 passengers per hour per direction, thus effectively bridging the gap between the maximum flow using buses and the minimum to justify a heavy metro. Its principal characteristics are steel-wheel rail vehicles, electrically-powered from an overhead wire system, and operated on a variety of rights-of-way. In comparison with the conventional railway, LRT is associated with shorter journeys, more frequent stops, less demanding construction parameters and considerably lighter vehicles. While in comparison with the bus LRT carries heavier loads more efficiently, quickly and reliably, with a substantial reduction in staffing levels, it does require more capital outlay than a bus system, but considerably less than a conventional rail system. There are some 300 cities and towns throughout the world in which LRT is in operation today and there are increasing numbers of locations where new LRT systems are being planned or built, often long after their tramways have been abandoned.

LRT has mainly developed in three ways, by modernising and upgrading street tramways converting and revitalising former short-distance rail services like the Tyne & Wear Metro or more recently by new construction. Although street tramways have declined in number since the 1930s in Europe, the particular concept of upgrading to LRT has been embraced with enthusiasm, providing the spur for interest throughout the world. It is now in North America that the greatest activity in this field is to be seen. All nine systems which survived until the 1980s have been modernised, three completely new systems have been opened, four more are being constructed and schemes are being developed in nine communities.

It must be remembered that LRT will provide a more substantial and therefore more accessible network than a heavy rail system. It should not be regarded as the exclusive mode as many LRT systems require bus feeders in suburban areas while in large cities LRT can act as the feeder to

The latest modern six-axle-articulated tramcar loading in Düsseldorf.

ordinary rail services. In Tyne & Wear bus services were recast to feed Metro stations at selected inchanges and cross city buses in Newcastle were withdrawn. Some areas with a population under 400,000 can justify LRT because of the local topography, while for new installations the existence of a suitable right of way serving the areas may well be the deciding factor. LRT can operate over a wide variety of rights-of-way with various degrees of segregation which can range from nil to 100 per cent on the same system. There is no clear dividing line between tramway, light rail transit and heavy rapid transit or metro, but it is reasonable to classify a light rail system as one where at least 40 per cent of the traffic is segregated from other traffic, while a true heavy metro requires 100 per cent segregation. Sections of unsegregated street track are acceptable where there is no cost effective alternative but these sections should be kept to a minimum if the advantages over buses are to be maintained. Where there is insufficient space for LRT tracks and other traffic, specific streets may be designated for LRT use while other are reserved for normal road traffic. LRT/pedestrian precincts are widely used in West Germany and are more satisfactory than bus/pedestrian precincts because of the predictable nature of the vehicle movement.

Street tracks can be segregated simply by white lines, cross-hatching, or more satisfactorily by raised kerbs which may be crossed by other vehicles in an emergency. At busy junctions it is better to segregate completely where possible in order to maintain the capacity of an LRT line or the intersecting highway and the LRT can be depressed into a short subway, perhaps with a stop reached by pedestrian ways, or elevated on to a viaduct. An LRT bridge can be quite attractive when constructed in modern concrete and considerably slimmer than that required by a four

lane highway or even a busway. Whereas 10 years ago planners were thinking of putting extensive sections of LRT systems underground at city centres, it is now widely accepted that for reasons of cost and accessibility public transport should retain its surface alignment wherever possible and the capacity of the system maintained by constraints on other categories of traffic.

Undoubtedly the ideal alignment for an LRT line is the median-strip which divides the dual-carriageway, with various degrees of sophistication, as this permits high speeds. An important consideration is that LRT can be operated over existing railway rights-of-way, either abandoned or under-utilised or indeed, taken over as was done by Tyneside's new LRT.

Reliable folding step mechanisms have been developed so that the LRT vehicle can pick up or set down passengers at either a simple platform halt or at street level.

There is often an illogical reaction against public transport stops being located in the centre of a highway, whether protected or otherwise, but it must be understood that whereas this requires 100 per cent of the passengers having to cross 50 per cent of the street, a kerbside stop will, using the same logic, require 50 per cent of the passengers having to cross 100 per cent of the street! In mainland Europe many loading points for LRT are located in the centre of the road on a miniature 'island-pavement' alongside the tracks access to which is gained by a pedestrian crossing, controlled or otherwise depending on the density of the other road traffic. The passengers then wait on this island-pavement until the LRT car arrives.

LRT can be inserted into the urban environment relatively easily because of its ability to cope with sharp curves and steep gradients. Minimum curve radius for LRT standard gauge track is 18m (60ft) compared with 40m (132ft) on old metros and 200m (660ft or 10 chains) on a heavy railway. Gradients of 8 per cent or 1 in 12 are common on tramways and 12 per cent is possible. Most LRT